The Puritan Impulse

HISTORY TOPIC BOOKS

General Editor: G. M. D. HOWAT,
   Head of the History Department, Radley College, Oxfordshire

The Puritan Impulse (1559–1660) M. M. REESE
Economy and Community (1500–1700) ROSEMARY O'DAY
The European Dynamic (1450–1715) MARGARET SHENNAN

BY THE SAME AUTHOR:

The Tudors and Stuarts
The Cease of Majesty
Shakespeare: his world and his work
William Shakespeare
ed., Elizabethan Verse Romances
ed., Gibbon's *Autobiography*
ed., British History Documents, 1485–1688
ed., British History Documents, 1688–1815

THE PURITAN IMPULSE

The English Revolution, 1559–1660

M. M. REESE

Adam & Charles Black
London

FIRST PUBLISHED 1975
A. & C. BLACK LTD
4, 5 & 6 SOHO SQUARE, LONDON W1V 6AD

© 1975 M. M. REESE

ISBN 0 7136 1472 2

PRINTED IN GREAT BRITAIN BY
HAZELL WATSON AND VINEY LTD
AYLESBURY, BUCKS

Contents

Introduction

This series, of which M. M. Reese's book forms a part, is intended for students working in the sixth form or at undergraduate level. The authors were asked to assume that their readers had a basic foundation in the sixteenth and seventeenth centuries. The manner of approach is intended to be thought-provoking, and to invite discussion. The extracts which accompany the arguments may be read both in relation to the text and in their own right. Numbers in square brackets are used to identify the extracts which are all placed at the end of the book.

G. M. D. HOWAT

Preface

The drama of a civil war and a king's execution has sometimes obscured the fact that the real work of the 'English Revolution' was accomplished in the months before the war began, when most of the significant groups in the country united to resist a style of government which they regarded as inimical to their own and the nation's interest. They asserted the supremacy of common law by abolishing the prerogative courts. They ensured the Crown's dependence on Parliament by outlawing its sources of extraordinary revenue and passing the Triennial Act. The virulence of the attack on royal servants seemed to include the whole court, and not just individual ministers, in the condemnation of unpopular policies; and the powers of the Crown were further threatened by proposals to abolish episcopacy and to establish Parliament's authority over ministers and the militia. Not least, radical elements in London were preparing to destroy the economic monopoly of the City companies.

The aim was decentralisation, to ensure the gentry's right to determine political and religious policy through Parliament and the agencies of common law. It reversed the continental trend towards bureaucratic despotism. But interference with the traditional machinery of government created a power vacuum and the consequent problem of filling it. The programme of the Grand Remonstrance finally disrupted the unity of the opposition, and various accidental causes, such as rebellion in Ireland, the importunity of the Scots and a general lack of statesmanship, led to a war which sober men on both sides regarded as the suicide of a generation. So for a few years Cromwell's guns articulated God's design for England, until the gains of 1641 were substantially confirmed at the Restoration.

In a recent book, *The Causes of the English Revolution* (London, 1972), Professor Lawrence Stone has argued that these causes were so diverse and cumulative that it would be unhistorical to claim a predominating importance for any of them. The strands are too intricately woven to be unravelled. But it may still be useful, he suggests, to examine particular causes in detail, as long as we do not lose sight of their interdependence or imply that in thus isolating them we are making them necessarily more significant than any other.

The purpose of this book is to examine the contribution of the Puritans. This was the theme of the nineteenth-century historian S. R. Gardiner, but subsequent emphasis on social and economic factors has made it no longer fashionable to regard the assault on the Stuart monarchy merely as one of the numinous achievements of the Reformed faith. Nor, on the other hand, were the Puritans just apocalyptic skinheads, however badly some of them behaved at King Charles I's trial, because the essential importance of the Puritan movement is to be found in the diffusion of its ideas into every corner of contemporary life.

There has not been space here for the proper development of some of the ideas suggested, and still less for detailed references or full supporting evidence. Books as short as this can best be justified if they provoke reasoned disagreement and guide the reader to other books.

M. M. REESE

1

What was a Puritan?

Heaven doth with us as we with torches do,
Not light them for themselves: for if our virtues
Did not go forth of us, 'twere all alike
As if we had them not: spirits are not finely touched
But to fine issues.

MEASURE FOR MEASURE I i 33

There is no better corrective of careless generalisations about 'cause' and 'effect' than A. F. Pollard's reminder that the Renaissance and the Reformation were goals as well as starting-points. In the continuity of Christian thought and practice there were at different times different degrees of emphasis, and even Luther's protest might initially be regarded—and by the Pope was so regarded—as another tiny movement in the constant swing of the theological pendulum. When Luther claimed authority for certain ideas about faith and grace, he was making an Augustinian's thrust at the Dominican ascendancy which had existed since Aquinas established that all the great Christian truths were demonstrable to reason; although this ascendancy had already been breached when two English Franciscans, Duns Scotus and William of Ockham, had found certain Christian mysteries, even the Mass itself, to be impenetrable by reason and therefore dependent on the believer's blind acceptance. In the quest to marry the visible to the invisible the mediaeval Church was seldom still, and it is possible to view the Reformation in quite contrary ways. It may be seen as a fatal tilting of the doctrinal balance, showing that Rome's many-horsed chariot had driven off the road at last. In another sense it was the last great fruit of mediaeval piety.

So before we speak of English Puritanism as being the 'cause' of anything, we have to remember that its beliefs and attitudes were much older than the sixteenth century. Paul and Augustine had preached the irresistibility of predestined grace and had seen the Church as a community of the elect. The ethical sternness of the early friars was impatient of sacraments and hierarchies and sought salvation through the leading of a good

Christian life. In its domestic roots Puritanism was always strong in areas that had been centres of Lollardy, and it was nourished from continental sources through the immigrants who arrived under Edward VI and the Englishmen who fled from Mary I. This two-way exchange introduced the evangelising influence of Calvin. The 'great men' of history have mostly been the representative men, people with gifts above the ordinary but synthesists rather than originators. By the clarity of his intellect and the single-mindedness of his purpose Calvin concentrated in his own person a particular set of ideas that fulfilled the aspirations of his age.

What, then, was a Puritan? It is difficult to find a definition neither so broad as to be meaningless nor so narrow as to exclude many who would have acknowledged the name. Analogies are dangerous, but we should have a similar problem in trying to define a Socialist today. Puritans and Socialists are, of course, quite different creatures, but the point of the analogy is that both groups comprehend a heterogeneous body of supporters who have general aims in common but do not all share the same passions or favour the same solutions. All large popular movements lose something of their original fervour and integrity when they are joined by the unscrupulous and the ambitious, the mean and the mad, the intransigents who are beyond the reach of rational discussion. Thus many people joined the Puritan movement for secular purposes and supported it only so far as it assisted their personal objectives; but at such times they spoke its language, and it cannot be said that they were not Puritans. Like modern Socialists, the Puritans had a recognisable identity, and despite the recurring difficulty of classifying particular men at particular moments, it is possible to know who they were and what they wanted.

The term was originally applied to men who insisted upon absolute purity of worship, the 'precisians' who objected to robes and ceremonies that reminded them of the Roman Antichrist. Initially it was a term of mockery and abuse, and to non-sympathisers it was always so. Well into the seventeenth century Puritans themselves were repudiating it as a smear inflicted on them by the Papists, and the contemporary Mrs Hutchinson in her memoirs of the life of Colonel Hutchinson complained that the enemies of godliness used it in an exaggerated way to ridicule everything they disliked [1]. There was endless name-throwing, in the dreariest style of our own contemporary politics, with the opprobrium earned by the fanatics being levelled at 'any man that beareth but the face of honesty'. Eventually the Puritans' opposition to Arminianism was identified with resistance to court policies as a whole. Puritanism by then had a definitely political connotation, and the Grand Remonstrance (1641) accused the Papists of applying it to all who wanted to 'preserve the laws and liberties of the kingdom, and to maintain religion in the power of it'. But for two generations it was a portmanteau term to contain many different attitudes, and the historian's best consolation is that contemporaries had as many difficulties with it as he has himself.

Stripped of these confusions, a Puritan was one who sought to establish 'the godly community', to realise here and now the Kingdom of God. The agents for this work were those whom God had predestined as his elect, the only necessary organisation was the presbytery prescribed in Scripture and adopted in the primitive Church, and all that might be needed in the way of amplification, commentary or interpretation was to be found in Calvin's *Institutes*. This may seem a crude simplification, but the Puritan's view of life was not complex. Although in practice it might be modified in response to local conditions in England or any other country where it had a footing, this was the pure Calvinism of Geneva, and it was an incomparable instrument for changing society.

Predestination was the driving force. In the extreme view of this doctrine as taught by Calvin, man was hopelessly corrupted by the fall. Among other refreshing comparisons, he was 'ordure', 'a rat scrambling pell-mell in the straw', and he had no hope of regeneration through society since no human institution was proof against the sin of Adam. But by His son's sacrifice God had been persuaded to redeem certain chosen people to salvation, and through them He would work for the establishment of His kingdom. These elect were not to withdraw into monastic seclusion nor, like the Anabaptists, abandon the world in small groups of persecuted believers. They were chosen for a purpose, the fulfilment of God's plan, and much of the energising force of the Elizabethan Puritans is explained by their conviction that they had work to do in the world.

Many of them believed, too, that the new Jerusalem was near at hand. Long ago God had made a covenant with Abraham and his people, but Israel had faltered in its mission. Then the apostles had been disappointed in their expectation of an imminent coming, but these hopes had been re-born with the optimism of the Reformation period. If Rome were the Antichrist whose reign had to precede man's final regeneration, the elect must put themselves in constant readiness. 'It is the work of the day to give God no rest till he sets up Jerusalem as the praise of the whole world.' This Jerusalem, moreover, was to be peculiarly English. With splendid insularity the Puritan expected God's kingdom to be planted not only in his own generation but in his own country. 'Who is a God like ours?' Cromwell was to ask; and again after the battle of Dunbar, 'We pray you own this people more and more; for they are the chariots and horsemen of Israel. . . . Shine forth to other nations, who shall emulate the glory of such a pattern'. 'God revealed Himself, as His manner is, first to us,' Milton wrote in 1643, and this conviction coloured all his political writings.

Election, however, was the privilege of the few, and this exclusiveness helped to give Puritanism its terrifying fervour. Adopting Augustine's theory of prevenient grace, Calvin taught that in the beginning God predestined certain people to salvation, and the rest were damned eternally. This election was regardless of God's foreknowledge of merit or good works in the recipient, and likewise no man to whom it had been refused could earn grace. For the chosen, grace was irresistible and could never be forfeited, and to such people was imputed, through His sacrifice, the righteousness of Christ. Calvin's premise was the absolute sovereignty of God, and we, who stagger under the burden of sin, are not to say that He is arbitrary or cruel, because our finite minds have no knowledge of His purpose. Free will does not enter into it, because without grace the human will is just a sodden mess. The Puritan John Preston said quite simply that the majority of mankind are reprobated to eternal damnation because God 'passes by some men before they have done either good or evil, and being vessels of wrath by sin are destinated to destruction, that the anger and power of God may be made known'.

A belief in predestination was held in some degree by most Englishmen of the time, even by those on the opposite side in the religious quarrel. Richard Hooker and James I accepted it, and when in 1595 a Cambridge divine suggested in a sermon that Christ died sufficiently for all, Archbishop Whitgift gathered his bishops at Lambeth to draw up an uncompromising defence of predestination [2]. The difference between the Puritans and the official Church was over worship rather than doctrine.

At the same time it is puzzling that hundreds of men and women should have been content to live quietly in the assurance of their own salvation, without worrying overmuch about their neighbours, while for others the idea of election should have had such an extraordinary force. It is true that it worked more strongly among the first generation of Puritans, those who had direct contact with continental Protestantism in the years between Henry VIII and Elizabeth I. But, as in so many of the dogmatic disputes of the sixteenth century, the difference was mainly one of emphasis. The convinced Puritan saw chiefly the power and mightiness of God, while Protestants of a milder temper acknowledged also His reasonableness and love. Ultimately it is a matter of the human equation rather than doctrinal certainty. Not everyone has the hardiness of spirit to be cast about by the viewless winds, and it was recognised that the severity of strict Calvinism could lead some men to antinomianism and despair. The seventeenth of the Thirty-Nine Articles is characteristically oblique on this. It begins by asserting predestination in terms any Puritan would accept, declaring God's choice to have been effected 'before the foundations of the world were laid', and election itself to be of 'sweet, pleasant, and unspeakable comfort to godly persons'. But this is balanced by concern for 'curious and carnal persons, lacking the Spirit of Christ', who, deprived of grace, are thrust 'either into desperation, or into wretchlessness of most unclean living, no less perilous than desperation'.

In a Calvinist community such persons were not allowed to languish in uncleanness or despair, because they were disciplined by the virtuous. Sceptics often asked how the saved were to be recognised, and Calvin himself had three answers to this. They were to be known by their sincere profession of faith; by participation in the sacrament as a sign of spiritual communion with God, 'a kind of mutual contract by which the Lord conveys His mercy to us, and by it eternal life, while we in our turn promise Him obedience'; and thirdly by the pursuit of holy living. Good deeds were an irrefutable sign of right belief, because if election to grace prescribed a certain standard of conduct, that conduct must be taken as a presumption of grace. The Calvinist was obviously open here to suspicion of arguing in a circle, but the proposition belongs to faith rather than reason and Puritanism can only be understood through acceptance of its own convictions. It was impossible for a man born in grace to lead other than an exemplary life, even though, being but mortal, he might fall into backslidings that earned the censure of the congregation and the temporary withdrawal of God's favour. He would also be successful in his worldly dealings, because he would have the sinews for the higher spiritual struggle and in his material concerns he would be provided for. It was impossible, likewise, for the damned to lead a godly life or even to prosper materially. But their sin and despair must not be allowed to fester as an affront to God, and although they could not help themselves, their errors had to be corrected by a godly discipline in order that the holy community, which was God's final purpose, might be presently established.

Inspired by a literal interpretation of God's word as revealed in Scripture, this was basically the theological system by which the English Puritan was guided to truth and holy living, and it armed him with a conviction always eager to challenge rulers, laws or institutions which came in his path. In many ways it was a harsh and disagreeable creed, merciless to failure. It could easily degenerate into a gospel of worldly success in which poverty was the result of debauchery and lack of thrift. The Puritan saw a clear pattern of personal responsibility, and he would have had no comprehension of the modern Therapeutic State where wrongdoing is merely the result of 'social allergies'. Thus his enemies found much to ridicule in the combination of acquisitiveness with ostentatious piety, the breast-beating and tendency to pharisaic display, the Biblical allusions and constant invocations of the Psalmist, the personal gluttony that was thought to accompany intolerance of other men's 'cakes and ale'. The principal charge was hypocrisy, the difference between recognising the moral law and steadfastly obeying it, and contemporaries were bitter about the 'counterfeit elect' whose piety seemed to be only a camouflage for pride and ambition. Nothing infuriated men more than the Puritan's 'airy fancies and presumption of being in acceptance with God'. Under the veil of His word, Elizabeth said, the Puritan was 'overbold with God Almighty'.

The Puritan was immature in his habit of personalising his temptations and his spiritual foes, and Puritan allegory was nearly always child-like and distasteful. On a more serious level, Puritanism could be accused of reducing Jesus to an agent in the mechanism of salvation; and by treating grace as an issue that was arbitrarily settled before the world began, the doctrine of predestination was ultimately inimical to the central purpose of religion—the knowledge and love of God. It refused to fallen man any natural will to goodness: 'I know that in me, that is, in my flesh, dwelleth no good thing'. But it is more hopeful to believe that the seed of God is in man and thus to know the wonder of the morning when the corn becomes orient and immortal wheat.

On the other hand, there was nothing enervating about Puritan fatalism. It bred men of strong nerves with a taste for liberty and the rights of private judgment; and although in its uncompromising conditions it denied the 'justification by works' that all the Protestant reformers hated, it took religion from the cloister and canalised man's productive energies to God's service. Society, by this rule, should be as Edmund Burke later desired it, something more than 'a partnership agreement in a trade of pepper and coffee'. Luther similarly had taught that 'the sphere of the operations of faith is the society of the world and its ordering', and the social conscience of the Puritans rescued many men from triviality, dissipation and the *accidie* (or lack of purpose) which some mediaeval thinkers had rebuked as the deadliest of the seven sins. The martyrologist John Foxe was exaggerating less than usual when he likened the godly preachers to the friars in their struggle against avarice and corruption.

Nor was the doctrine of predestination wholly unsound psychologically. No doctrine could have won such sustained and widespread support that did not correspond in some way to men's daily experience of the world, and in every generation there have been some who have presented themselves to their fellows as innately good and others who have seemed to be beyond redemption. Calvin was no more uncompromising than Machiavelli in his certainty of man's natural disposition to wickedness and predatory self-interest, and a furtive acceptance of Machiavelli's leaden truths was one of the dominant influences of the sixteenth century. Calvin at least offered a more hopeful solution than Machiavelli's schemes for meeting evil with a worse evil.

The Puritans, then, saw the Church as an instrument to sanctify society to the glory of God. Restless under the heavy weight of sin, they felt themselves to be bound in a covenant with God to a holy life enforced through a discipline exercised by the congregation. In this way they hoped to erect in England the City of God whose statutes and ordinances were to be found in Scripture and nowhere else. This was not an ignoble purpose, and it is a plain historical fact that this moral and spiritual idea took the place in England of the charismatic personal leadership that for some reason the native island Reformation did not produce. The hour does not always bring forth the man. To the individual this idea brought an exalting sense of his personal value in the vast, unending warfare for the soul of man. But at the same time it transcended his personal value and made him one whose virtues went forth from him, a torch whom God had lighted for His own intents. The Puritan lived by faith to the glory and service of God in a world which he was called by his elected grace to bring from carnal disorder to the long-promised blessedness. Sceptics have found an element of self-deception in this, but it was an aristocratic conception of life.

For its fulfilment Calvin found all the necessary agencies in Scripture, and it was here, when they urged their formula too precisely, that the English Puritans came into conflict with authority. In reaction against the supposed perversions of Rome, all the Reformed faiths put their confidence in Scripture, substituting for an infallible Church and tradition an infallible Word and a liberty to disagree about its meaning. The Reformers found in the Bible not only an impregnable statement of belief but a prescription for the only possible organisation of the Christian Church, although this might be supplemented from the recorded practice of the first believers. This testimony was all the more powerful because Protestants thought that in the dark mediaeval centuries it had been deliberately perverted by the Pope.

If there ever was such a thing as a canonical Calvinism, an absolute, unvarying orthodoxy, it was in Geneva; where, however, there was always questioning and opposition, and Calvin himself did not become a citizen until 1556. Elsewhere his followers would adapt their ideas and procedure to local conditions, although even this, as in England, led to disputes among themselves. But Calvinists as a recognisable body were united on what they regarded as essential, and basically they were agreed in tolerating 'things indifferent', matters of doctrine, worship or organisation that were not immediately necessary to right living, until opportunity came to reform them.

Ministers in the Calvinist communions were variously nominated, elected or approved by their congregations, and they underwent a non-sacramental ordination that was a contract between their people and themselves. The controversial issue was the spiritual function of the 'presbyter'. It was held that in the early Church the presbyter, which could simply mean an elder or a ruler, a man elevated by experience and wisdom, exercised all the powers and rights of the Christian ministry including ordination. There was then no order superior to this, all ministers being equal by virtue of their common commission to do Christ's work until His promised return, then believed to be imminent; and bishop, which means *episcopus* or overseer, was just an interchangeable term for presbyter. Gradually, however, the moderator, who was the presiding officer of the local assembly of clergy and deacons, was allowed to assume supervisory powers over a wide area and relegate the presbyter, or ordinary minister, to a secondary place in the priesthood. This was, allegedly, the origin of prelacy and the usurped authority of bishops. Richard Baxter, a nonconformist divine who alternated fundamentalist obscurantism with endearing fits of moderation and common sense, argued that Christ delegated to the presbyter His three attributes of prophet, priest and king. By episcopal intrusion the presbyter had been deprived of his 'kingly' function as a ruler of the congregation, and where his administrative duties were performed by professional lawyers in the ecclesiastical courts, there was no true Christian Church.

In Geneva Calvin divided the duties of presbyter between the ministers, who were to preach and teach, and the elders, who were responsible for discipline and administration. This was the system adopted in his lifetime in the Reformed communities of Switzerland, Scotland and France, and it remained to be seen whether it would be adopted also in England, where the traditional forms of episcopacy had survived the early stages of the Reformation.

2

Tarrying for the Magistrate

Wherein I'll catch the conscience of the king.

HAMLET II ii 635

Following the accession of Elizabeth I in 1558, the Marian fugitives returned to England with the dangerous zeal of first-generation converts sharpened by a sense of grievance. In some there was also a sense of shame that their brethren in England had suffered death while they themselves sought the comparative safety of the Continent. The need to appease their consciences may partly explain the contentious stridency of their return.

During their exile their behaviour had often been noisy and full of dispute. The famous quarrel of Cox and Knox at Frankfurt broke out again between Horne and Whitehead, and there were similar differences over religious usage in Strasburg, Basle and Wesel. Their travels made them conscious of the inevitable fragmentation of the Reformed faiths, and they were by no means of one mind about doctrine and worship when Mary I's death allowed them to return to England. What united them was their conviction that England must be brought to the true and godly Reformation that had been lacking hitherto. In the eyes of all advanced reformers England was an important prize, because their continental experiences had made them aware of the vulnerability of their cause. Most of the German cities had settled into an obdurate Lutheranism, and because of their Calvinist opinions John à Lasco and his attendant evangels had been refused admission to places like Hamburg, Weimar and Lübeck. Nor could the reformers feel assured of the continuing security of their faith in the Swiss towns, tiny places with a long history of political change and alien domination. Calvin himself was an exile, and Geneva in his time was constantly threatened with re-occupation by its former rulers. (A few years later the Duke of Alva, when on his way to the Netherlands, thought of breaking his journey to

17

sack the place.) The Augsburg Interim of 1548 had put all conscientious Protestants in danger, and in the Peace of 1555 Lutheranism was the only heterodox system to be officially recognised. Thus the returning fugitives were watched from abroad as missionaries of a cause spiritually impregnable but politically brittle, and this close continental attachment was one of the controlling influences in early English Puritanism. Soon after he has become Bishop of Salisbury, Jewel is writing to Peter Martyr, 'my father and my pride', and he sends his salutations to 'Masters Gualter, Simler, Lavater, Haller, Gesner, Frisius, Herman'.

In the immediate issue of royal supremacy and doctrinal definition the reformers won ground from Queen Elizabeth and her council. William Cecil, the Queen's minister, who had stayed at home and watched it all, had a scheme of conciliation for drawing men of all persuasions into a moderate and embracing system, but this had to be modified in the face of parliamentary opposition which did not come only from the bishops in the House of Lords. The existence of a Puritan ideology in the Commons, as yet vague but later to become formalised and articulate, was evident already. The Coxians prevailed against Knox, who went to Scotland to be borne to power on a tide of piety and plunder, but the settlement of 1559 was a partial government defeat. This was to be the pattern of the reign, one of royal initiatives which won occasional victories and always avoided a formal retreat but conceded over the years many semi-surrenders, often in a different area of conflict. Thus, by 1600 the original position had been dangerously undermined.

The reformers viewed the settlement as ground gained for a further advance. They had little sympathy with the official policy of temporising with the Catholics, since the best defence against error was a total commitment to the truth. The severe mortality among bishops in 1558–9 seemed a clear sign from heaven, and it decimated an episcopate which, given time, would have brought to England the revived scholarship and piety of the Counter-Reformation. Except Kitchin of Llandaff, who 'smacked of the willow rather than the oak', the survivors all resigned, so that the first generation of Elizabethan bishops necessarily included several with personal experience of the continental scene—Cox, Jewel, Grindal, Sandys, Horne, Scory, Pilkington, Parkhurst, Nicholas Bullingham, Berkeley, Davies, Bentham and Young. Others had spent the past reign in self-effacing concealment, like Alley of Exeter, who had led a twilight existence as a teacher of science in the north of England. Most of these men felt that in taking office they were compounding a spiritual error, and at best they could only regard it as an administrative convenience. It was perhaps a tragedy for all parties that Cranmer did not live to launch the Elizabethan Church in a spirit of moderation and respect for tradition. In all his doctrinal waverings he did not lose sight of his conception of *Ecclesia Anglicana* as a continuing national Church, now spiritually reformed but still a member of an enduring Christian polity.

The Puritan reformers made an immediate assault on what Ben Jonson's Tribulation Wholesome called 'the menstruous cloth and rag of Rome'. In the Injunctions of 1559 and the controversial Ornaments Rubric the government probably intended to prescribe such ceremonial observances as would, without fostering superstition, make it possible for Catholics to go to church. But these outward symbols were thought by the Puritans to have no warrant in Scripture and to be devices by which the Romish clergy had exploited the credulity of simple men. It had been difficult to persuade Hooper to put on a surplice for his consecration as Bishop of Gloucester; and now Coverdale, one of the officiating bishops, appeared at Matthew Parker's consecration as Archbishop of Canterbury in a long grey dressing-gown, and Cox was refusing to preach in the Queen's chapel because of the crosses and candles she maintained there. Jewel reported to his continental friends that 'the scenic apparatus of divine worship is now under agitation', and in 1562 it was only by a massive use of proxies that the lower house of Convocation rejected a programme inspired by Sandys, then Bishop of Worcester, demanding that organs and the sign of the cross in baptism be removed from the services, kneeling at Communion be left to the ordinary's discretion, and the surplice be a sufficient vestment for all the clergy's ministrations. With most of the bishops hostile to the law and unwilling to enforce it, William Cecil called for reports and was alarmed at what he found [3].

The vestments controversy was damped down by Matthew Parker's *Book of Advertisements* (1566). At a distance it may seem trivial, but it was not trivial to men who regarded ceremonies as an offence to God on the eve of His coming to judge the righteous. It mattered also to ordinary men who were mistrustful of any concession to the Roman adversary, and Puritanism attracted lay support for this reason. Puritan agitation should always be considered against the background of international events: the Catholic revival at Trent, the ubiquitous advance of the Jesuits, Alva in the Netherlands, the Huguenot defeats in 1569 at Jarnac and Moncontour, the Northern Earls and the other conspiracies for Mary Queen of Scots, Elizabeth's excommunication, the massacre of St Bartholomew, the Spanish acquisition of Portugal, the assassination of William the Silent. The demand for reform was always loudest when the clouds were dark outside. 'Protestantism in danger' was a cry that never failed.

The reforming movement was further stimulated by the behaviour of the Queen. Personally, Elizabeth clung to her crosses and candles as secular people do when they are looking for religion to have some meaning for them. As a sovereign she was conscious of her duty to reconcile one half of her people with the other, and for this purpose she had to insist upon the ecclesiastical supremacy of the Crown. Neither Rome nor Geneva should have any pretensions here, but whereas the issue with Rome was clear-cut, the Puritan problem was double-edged. In Protestant theory 'tarrying for the magistrate' meant a process of patient conversion until the godly prince should acknowledge the light that was in him by the very fact of his institution. Calvinism was equivocal about this, and it is beside the point to say that it was either Erastian or 'popular'. Ideally, Church and State were one, as in Geneva they actually were. But Geneva was a special case: a community of about 6,000 whose population was rather more than doubled by the prestigious influence of Calvin. An appearance of seamless unity was established by the excommunication, coercion or expulsion of the recalcitrant. When in other countries the faithful had to struggle for recognition, Calvin recommended a policy of co-operation and obedience while the magistrate was persuaded to conform. He acknowledged, however, that there would be occasions when the lesser magistrate would have to correct or disobey the higher—when, in the English context, Parliament would have to correct the Crown—and it was this permission to resist supreme authority that earned Calvinism its widespread reputation as 'the religion of insurrection'. Implicit in this was the belief in the 'parity' or equality of ministers. In itself this was just a clerical theory whose supposed derivation from Scripture was open to question, but a challenge to the hierarchy of the Church must, in the tight-knit interdependence of the institutions of sixteenth-century government, also involve the political hierarchy. James I at the start of his reign had put it succinctly, 'No bishop, no king'. Laud, in a sermon preached before Parliament in 1626, expressed it more elaborately: 'They, whoever they be, that would overthrow *sedes ecclesiae*, the seats of ecclesiastical government, will not spare (if ever they get power) to have a pluck at the throne of David'.

Elizabeth was in no mind to be the pliable magistrate of Puritan expectation. She had to preserve a comprehensive settlement to retain Catholic loyalty, she was temperamentally antipathetic to Puritans and, above all, she was jealous of her constitutional prerogative. She was already having brushes with the Commons about marriage, the succession and other matters, and she felt that it would be dangerous to allow herself to be pushed off course by parliamentary pressure over religion. Like any other ruler, she saw the inherent threat in Calvinist doctrine. But it was always her policy to avoid confrontation where she could, and hope that her problems would quietly disappear. Puritanism did not disappear, and that was one of her miscalculations. In the belief that it would, she left repression to the bishops, whom she expected to exercise the powers delegated to them under the royal supremacy. This was a ridiculous policy, since most of them were in sympathy with the activities they were required to suppress, but in fairness to her she did not get much support from her council in this matter. Among her closest advisers, Leicester (for the sake of popularity rather than conviction), Walsingham, Knollys, Mildmay (who founded Emmanuel College at Cambridge to be a Puritan seminary) and even William Cecil were sympathetic to many of the Puritan demands.

The burden fell on Matthew Parker, a meek and scholarly man who never wanted to be archbishop and would have been happier in the company of his books and his splendidly resolute wife. His own position was that he did not give a jot for tippet, fur cap and wafer-bread, but he disliked 'Germanical natures' and he thought the law should be respected. He did his best to bring the bishops to a sense of duty and he deprived a number of clergy in London, where Grindal, their bishop, was being characteristically vague and indulgent. But Parker's *Book of Advertisements* caused the first schism in the Church, simply on the issue of vestments, and it was soon followed by a more serious attack on the Prayer Book and the episcopal office. Parker was forced to the battle-front, a reluctant Uriah, without adequate support from the rear. 'I have little help (if ye knew all) where I thought to have most,' he commented in a letter to a fellow bishop. Elizabeth sought to control the Church through the prerogative vested in her by the Act of Supremacy, and she expected the bishops to establish uniformity through their own ecclesiastical courts. Because she did not recognise Parliament's right to interfere, she rejected the bishops' claim that their task would be easier if doctrine and worship were prescribed by statute. She foiled the Commons' efforts in the 1560s to proceed with the reformation of canon law that had been started under Edward VI, and she managed to hold off until 1571 their pressure to give statutory force to the Thirty-Nine Articles. Reputedly, a significant phrase in Article 20, 'The Church hath power to decree rites and ceremonies and authority in controversies of faith', was her own addition. Anxious to avoid personal intervention, she compelled the bishops to enforce an unpopular policy while at the same time undermining their authority by publicly rebuking them for being lax and ineffective. She harassed Parker about clerical marriage, including his own, and probably the only churchman in her reign she did not despise was Whitgift, her 'little black husband', who was no one's husband in the flesh and was a statesman rather than an ecclesiastic. By compelling the bishops to seem to be opponents of reform, she exposed them to attacks on the validity of their office.

Meanwhile support for the Puritans was widened by the manifest disorders in the Church which seemed to call for the godly discipline which they recommended. In a visitation in his Gloucester diocese in 1551 Hooper claimed that, of 311 clergy examined, 10 could not say the Lord's Prayer, 27 did not know who first spoke it and 30 did not know where they might find it. Hooper was given to exaggeration, but there was a broad truth in this picture. Parish records of the sixteenth century reveal an extraordinary readiness among incumbents to stay at their posts through all the changes of the period. (At Weobley in Herefordshire, for instance, only three rectors were instituted between 1492 and 1611, which perhaps is an extreme case.) As a body the parochial clergy were torpid and unenlightened men, and their virtue was in qualities the Puritans did not much esteem. As well as spiritual guides of limited qualification they were the parish men-of-all-work, farmers, doctors, vets, legal advisers, craftsmen, musicians, teachers. Shakespeare's Sir Nathaniel in *Love's Labour's Lost* was an honest man, a good neighbour and a good bowler. Such men were not unfulfilled. By 1600 their moral and intellectual standard was much improved, and Puritan zeal has some credit for this, but the principal reason was clerical marriage, which, next to the distribution of monastic land, was the great vested interest of the Reformation. It gave the parson roots and responsibility lacking to him in a celibate condition.

But in the 1560s, the ordinary clergy were ignorant and obdurately willing to continue so. There were not enough of them—one parish in five had no resident priest—they were absurdly underpaid, and patrons were indifferent to the quality of the men they appointed. The Church's basic weakness was lay impropriations. Of a total of more than 9,000 parishes 41 per cent were owned by laymen or corporations who had bought the tithe (the tenth of their annual produce contributed by parishioners to the maintenance of their priest) and paid a wage to the vicar to look after the parish. This wage could be as low as 15 per cent of the value of the living, and Grindal understandably complained that 'exility of stipends' was the great obstacle to the provision of a qualified priesthood. Impropriation was a recognised commercial speculation, and

Shakespeare was typical of the rising *rentier* class when in 1605 he paid £440 for a lease of about a quarter of the tithes in Stratford. The investment was bringing in £90 a year when his heirs sold the lease to the corporation twenty years later. In 1563 Cecil introduced a bill to tax impropriations to provide adequate clerical stipends, but this, like similar proposals in the following years, was defeated as interference with the rights of property. On the other hand, the Puritans used impropriations to good effect by persuading well-disposed patrons to appoint, with augmented stipends, clergy known to be faithful to the cause. A parallel move was the appointment, often in the guise of private chaplains, of 'lecturers' to preach the authentic Word. A preaching ministry was the consuming spiritual hunger of the age, and the Puritans were able in the long run to transform Elizabethan life because, despite their failure to alter the official worship of the Church, they succeeded in capturing the pulpit. In a semi-literate age this was equivalent to the importance in modern times of 'controlling the media'.

The Puritans had already discovered that it was hopeless to expect reform from the bishops, many of whom were engaged in abuses as squalid as any that had prevailed before the Reformation. It was not wholly their fault, as Elizabeth and her courtiers cynically exploited the hierarchy to whom they looked for the proper government of the Church. The reason was the financial stringency of the Crown in an inflationary period, which will be discussed in the next section. As one of her expedients for remaining solvent the Queen had to plunder the revenues of the Church. It was nothing new: Latimer had complained of it, as of so much else, and Northumberland had even squeezed some episcopal manors from Hooper. Mary dutifully restored Church lands annexed to the Crown, but in 1559 an Act authorised the Crown to use the temporalities of a bishopric during a vacancy. It also channelled the disreputable traffic by decreeing that long leases of episcopal land were to be made only to the Crown, which was able to acquire rich manors in exchange for parcels of tithe. It was therefore to Elizabeth's advantage to keep sees vacant and this she frequently did. For a time in 1584 five sees had no bishop; Oxford was kept vacant for forty-one years and Bristol for fourteen in addition to being held *in commendam* with Gloucester for twenty-seven years. At Ely poor Cox was warned not to let the Queen discover 'how great a grazier, how marvellous a dairyman, how rich a farmer' he was, but he committed the mistake of being married, twice, and his rich see was plundered. He had to surrender his property at Holborn to Sir Christopher Hatton and in 1580 he resigned in vexation. For eighteen years the revenues were enjoyed by the bankrupt Earl of Oxford and a Portuguese pretender, and when at last a successor was appointed, it was on the condition of agreeing to further spoliation.

As the Crown also enjoyed a year's first-fruits of all ecclesiastical preferments, it paid Elizabeth to keep her bishops on the move, and some found themselves translated before they had discharged the debt on their first consecration. Yet there was no lack of competition for the richer prizes, and churchmen offered huge bribes in the quest for promotion, promising to alienate some of their richest manors. The bishopric of Salisbury was twice put up to auction. Some of the bishops saw no harm in these practices as they did not regard their offices as divinely ordained, and it was commonly believed that Parker would be the last archbishop. Their tenures were not hereditary, and so they took the opportunity to provide for their families while they could. Some, no doubt, also thought iconoclasm to be a religious duty. They sold timber, lead, shrines and ornaments, and for the bribes they had to pay to courtiers they recouped themselves from the profits of ecclesiastical jurisdiction and from the impropriation of parishes within their sees. In the Queen's defence, plundering the Church was one of the few viable means of providing salaries for men who devoted their lives to government service. But it led to pluralism and non-residence and an aggravation of all the abuses of which the Puritans complained. Convocation was always making well-meant gestures of reform, and the better bishops were careful to examine and instruct their clergy. But stipends continued to be a stumbling-block, and while about one-fifth of the parishes had no resident priest, there were qualified clergy who could not get livings because there was no money to pay them. In some dioceses it required goodwill and organisation to provide the people with one sermon a month, or even one every two months. With deans and chapters often behaving as greedily as the bishops, a rift developed between the hierarchy and the lesser clergy.

At the beginning of Elizabeth's reign most reformers had been content to look on episcopacy as a 'thing indifferent'. Like vestments, it could be endured for a while because in essentials the Church was a true Church. It was the same with the Prayer Book. Calvin found that it contained some Popish sludge, but its deviations from truth were 'endurable trifles'. A much stronger assault began when the Queen's conscience was found to be impervious to appeal, and the bishops' obstructiveness was being viewed in a more sinister light. It seemed that there could be no true reformation until they had been reduced to their right scriptural functions. The Puritans attempted to accomplish this reformation by parliamentary action. In 1571 Walter Strickland introduced a bill for a reform of the imperfections in the Prayer Book. He was whisked out of sight by the Queen's apparitors, but he had to be released, with some loss of face, and a conference between reformers and bishops ended with Peter Wentworth's angry threat to 'pass nothing before we know what it is. That were to make you popes'. His two bills in the following year were confiscated by the Queen, and the radical Puritans then proposed a more forthright policy in the first and second *Admonition to Parliament* [4]: the first by Field and Wilcox, two Puritan preachers, and the second by Thomas Cartwright, who after losing his Cambridge professorship in a dispute with Whitgift had been to Geneva and confirmed his opinion that here was to be found the perfect model for Christ's government.

The aim was to amend the Prayer Book, with its vain plea that all men might be saved, and to establish a system of worship conformable with God's Word, based on a ministry of pastors, elders and deacons all equal in the priesthood, and enforced by the discipline of the consistory. This was not an abandonment of the policy of tarrying for the magistrate, although it was designed to propel him in the way he ought to go. The Puritans were absolutely loyal to Elizabeth personally, if only because the likely alternatives were Philip of Spain or Mary Queen of Scots, and there was no question yet in anybody's mind of separating religion from politics or of sundering the indivisible unity of Church and State. This was still an attempt at reform from within. But it was too drastic for the time and place, and undiluted Presbyterianism, although successfully imposed in Scotland by the General Assembly, never made much headway in England. Even supposing that the Genevan system were founded on a correct interpretation of the Gospel, it was unhistorical to regard the precepts and practices of a small persecuted sect as a final institution, or to believe that they would not adapt themselves to changing conditions in time to come.

In 1574 Cartwright translated the *Book of Discipline* by Walter Travers, which was intended to replace the Prayer Book by a Directory of Public Worship. This was to be the structure of the *classis* system later (see page 27), but only a minority adopted it, and the Presbyterian plan divided the radical Puritans from the moderates. If bishops would use their powers reasonably and set a godly example, the moderates would accept an institution that was deeply entrenched in English society. The chief practical danger from Presbyterian ideas arose from their promise of further plunder. Many godly Puritans, not all of them convinced Presbyterians, so far forgot their principles as to bribe the laity with hopes of the confiscated wealth of the bishops, chapters and cathedrals. Many people thought that this was the real motive behind the demand for 'parity' [5], and Mrs Hutchinson was to admit later that the Puritans, 'being weak and oppressed, had not faith enough to disown all that adhered to them for worldly interests'. Shakespeare's Angelo in *Measure for Measure* took sombre note of the temptation that 'doth goad us on to sin, in loving virtue', but in Jonson's *The Alchemist* Tribulation Wholesome had a more convenient explanation. When the deacon Ananias protested that the sanctified cause should follow a sanctified course, he replied that all means might be used 'to give furtherance to the holy cause', and the children of perdition were often instruments of godly works. With the monasteries and chantries gone already, it was not illogical to demand that the episcopal estates should go too, as they already had in the Reformed communities of the Continent, where the Dutch were using the proceeds for the defence of their sea-threatened acres. The Puritans courted Leicester and Essex with the bait of all this wealth if they would lead a godly Reformation, and this programme was revived during John Preston's wooing of Buckingham in the 1620s; but episcopacy survived in England until the Scots made its abolition the price of their military alliance.

The Puritan preachers Field and Wilcox were assiduous in propaganda and subterranean organisation, and Wentworth continued to put religious bills before Parliament and complain that 'God was shut out of doors' when he was forbidden to discuss them. Elizabeth made it quite clear that she would not consider any changes not recommended by Convocation, and there was a recoil from the severity of Cartwright's system, so implacably rigid in its definitions. There was perhaps also some recoil from the man himself, with his demand that death be the penalty for heresy, blasphemy and adultery: and 'if this be bloody and extreme, I am content to be so counted with the Holy Ghost'. It was more agreeable to listen to Acontius, an Italian lawyer, philosopher and engineer who came to London to help reclaim some land inundated by the Thames. He was a Protestant who worshipped with one of the emigrant Dutch congregations, but he argued that a Church should not try to enforce matters which God had not specifically pronounced to be necessary. This was doing Satan's work for him, because it led to dissent and persecution and a weakening of faith.

The 'prophesyings' of the middle-seventies showed Puritanism at its best, in an attempt to establish the godly community by fertilisation from within. It had a touch of the pragmatic, but the intent was that the instructed few should leaven the doughy mass by discussion, persuasion and example until at length the country had a proper number of competent preachers. But laymen were often admitted to these exercises, and the commentaries on scriptural texts could become tendentious and touch on delicate matters of worship and Church government. The new Archbishop of Canterbury was Edmund Grindal, known to be of Puritan inclination. It was an extraordinary appointment for Elizabeth to have made at a critical time, but Cecil is believed to have urged it, and at least Grindal had been less ineffective at York, where he had kept a firm hand on the Catholics, than he had been earlier in London. He believed that prophesyings should be encouraged, with suitable safeguards against heretical propaganda, because they would eventually supply a preaching ministry and overcome pluralism and non-residence. Lack of money would have defeated this expectation anyway, but Grindal hoped that, with reform of the ecclesiastical courts, prophesyings would bring peace in the Church. Many of the bishops agreed with him and drew up regulations for the proper control of the exercises. They were supported also in the Privy Council, but rightly or wrongly the Queen decided that they must cease. She disliked preaching, with its opportunities for the dissemination of dangerous ideas, and she thought that the official Homilies contained all the edification the people needed. She ordered Grindal to suppress the prophesyings and received in reply a letter which indicated the Puritan view of her place in the scheme of things [6]. He could not be dismissed, as this would have conceded the argument that bishops were State appointments without any divine sanction, but he was virtually suspended until his death in 1583.

It has often been suggested that Elizabeth's failure to allow moderate Puritan reforms was the greatest blunder of her reign, and it was a Puritan who later described her as a sluttish housewife who merely swept her problems behind the door. But Cecil appointed Walter Travers to be his chaplain and tutor of his children, and this gives some idea of the difficulties she faced. 'Things indifferent' was a specious principle and, once conceded, they could become things essential. She had to keep the Catholics within the national Church and avoid the religious factions that were tearing France to pieces. Immediately she gained her point and the bishops broke up the prophesyings, but it was at some cost to them and her. A preacher told her that she was 'an untamed heifer, that would not be ruled by God's people, but obstructed His discipline'. After listing the abuses which disfigured the ministry and government of the Church, the Puritan Dering accused her of sitting idly by while 'all these whoredoms are committed'. Despairing of reform through the Queen or the bishops, the more determined Puritans set up the *classis* system, which was openly subversive. An outward pretence of conformity was maintained, and the element of lay discipline was exercised by men nominally appointed as churchwardens or collectors for the poor. A *classis* was a grouping or conference of neighbouring ministers who took Travers's *Book of Discipline* as their model, and periodically these groups would combine at a provincial synod. To coincide with meetings of Parliament national synods were held in London, and Field organised a massive campaign for the session of 1586. It was preceded by 'surveys' of the state of religion in the hands of ignorant, non-preaching, double-beneficed gamesters, drunkards and fornicators, and this exaggerated picture was used to lobby lay support in the Commons. In 1587 Sir Anthony Cope moved the repeal of the existing laws and the adoption of the *Book of Discipline* as the basis of public worship, but the House would not allow either the bill or the book to be introduced. The result of this failure was the series of Marprelate Tracts. The repetitious stupidity of these pamphlets makes it remarkable that anyone should have taken the considerable risk of secretly writing and printing them, but when the bishops were moved to reply in kind, the campaign certainly did nothing for their dignity and reputation [7].

The real object of the attack was Whitgift, who succeeded Grindal in 1583 and, brushing aside the Queen's hesitations and the opposition of the Privy Council (notably Robert Beale, their clerk, who fought him at every step), determined to force the Puritans to conform. He had Calvinist leanings himself, but he feared the political implications of the doctrine—'those which now impugn the ecclesiastical jurisdiction will endeavour also to impair the temporal, and to bring even kings and princes under their censure'—and the issue to his mind was not whether the Puritans were right but whether it stood 'with godly and Christian wisdom' to try to reconstruct the national Church in a time of external danger. He at once issued articles requiring all clergy to recognise the Crown's supremacy in religion and to acknowledge that the Prayer Book and the Thirty-Nine Articles contained nothing contrary to the Word of God. All the articles of 1583 had been laid down by Convocation on earlier occasions. The novelty was an archbishop who intended them to be observed. He compelled the clergy to subscribe and deprived them if they did not. His instrument was the prerogative court of High Commission, which had developed from the various ecclesiastical commissions issued under the royal supremacy; and, as the equivalent in the Church of the courts of Chancery and Star Chamber, private suitors found it quicker, fairer and cheaper than the traditional courts supervised by the bishops. But Whitgift used it as a political instrument to compel conformity, and particular objection was taken to the *ex officio* oath, a canon law procedure which could oblige a defendant to testify against himself. Cecil (now Lord Burghley) said, ineptly, that the court 'savoured of the Roman Inquisition', but he had a better point when he claimed that Whitgift's real purpose was not to reform religion but to hunt defaulters. Many clergy were suspended or deprived, and the Puritans complained that although Whitgift admitted that there was a deplorable lack of qualified preachers, he was deliberately silencing some of the most learned and eloquent. Deprivation also raised the delicate issue of property rights by threatening the parson's freehold, and in 1591 a test case was stage-managed for Robert Cawdrey, holder of one of Burghley's livings in Suffolk. Deprived for nonconformity, he sued his successor for trespass on the ground that an incumbent could not be deprived of his freehold except by statute or common law; but the judges ruled that the powers of High Commission were a lawful exercise of the Queen's prerogative in religion.

The circulation of the Marprelate libels in the year of the Spanish Armada helped to win some support for Whitgift, and the lay allies of Puritanism were further disquieted by the alarming assertions of the Separatists. In the long run Separatism was an inevitable expression of any creed based on the sovereignty of the individual conscience. The failure of tarrying for the magistrate, and the effectiveness of Whitgift's pedagogic discipline, combined with this inherent fragmentation of an individualistic religion to produce Robert Browne and his followers, who were for 'reformation without tarrying for any'. They founded the 'gathered' Churches, justifying themselves by the promise of Jesus that when two or three were gathered in His name, He would be in their midst. Rejecting a national Church, they proclaimed the sovereign independence of the individual congregation. They rapidly split and quarrelled among themselves over the exact nature of their scriptural dispensation, and they also attracted the free-wheelers—Anabaptists, the Family of Love, the Seekers, and the like—whose idiosyncrasy was well known on the Continent. In every Puritan, perhaps, there is a Muggletonian struggling to escape. The best of these men suffered ostracism and persecution with undeflected conviction, and it may be that they represented the Puritan ideal at its finest. Reunited only in 1972, the two main developments in nonconformity, Church-type and sect-type, were alternative approaches to the establishment of the godly community, and the sects abandoned hope of reforming a Church that compromised with time-servers and sinners.

They eased the way for Whitgift by frightening men of substance. In rejecting the ancient interdependence of Church and State they threatened the whole structure of the community. It was not just the bishops and their temporalities, which many men disliked anyway; the threat now was to the squire's advowson and his tithe, to law and property and the whole structure of 'degree' which appointed to each man his appointed place. The Separatists repudiated allegiance to any other authority but the congregation of believers. A fanatic called Hacket plotted to depose the Queen in readiness for his own enthronement as the Messiah; he and other intransigents were hanged as traitors to the peace of the realm, and in 1593 Parliament passed the savage Conventicle Act, significantly the first use of statute in Elizabeth's long struggle with Puritan dissent.

The hunt for the authors and printing-presses of the Marprelate Tracts uncovered alarming facts about Puritan intrigue, and Whitgift had clearly won his battle. It is sometimes said that this was the end of Puritanism until it was given new life by Stuart folly, but we have only to look at the Millenary Petition, or the demands of Parliament in 1604, to see that this was not so. The petition asked for the clergy to be relieved of subscription to Whitgift's articles, but in spirit it went back to Grindal in pleading for a learned preaching ministry (supported by stipends worth one-sixth or one-seventh of the value of lay impropriations), the reform of abuses, and the abolition of ceremonies that prevented the worshipper's immediate seeking after God. In proroguing Parliament after the session of 1604, James I similarly acknowledged the continuity of Puritanism when he expressed surprise that 'in three days after the beginning of the Parliament men should go contrary to their oaths of supremacy. . . . I did not think they had been so great, so proud or so dominant in your House. . . . In things that are against the Word of God I will with as great humility as any slave fall upon my knees or face; but in things indifferent they are seditious which obey not the magistrate'.

In the 1590s Puritanism was not dead but it was less immediately important. Embarrassed by the excesses of the extremists, moderate reformers were relieved when the *classes* were dispersed and the sectaries were persecuted or went into voluntary exile. The execution of Mary Stuart and the defeat of the Armada had cooled the patriotic fervour from which the Puritans, as guardians of the true faith, had gained so much support. It might perhaps have grown hot again if Essex had succeeded in his rising, that sad little coda to the reign. Essex's fault, according to Sir Robert Naunton in *Fragmenta Regalia* (1641), was to expect too much from the Queen too quickly: he 'drew in too fast, like a child sucking on an over-uberous nurse'. He might, if his wild gamble had succeeded, have courted a Puritan alliance. But the main concerns of this decade were financial and constitutional, and the ordinary Puritan could await the new reign in the comfortable knowledge of what silent revolution had already accomplished. Richard Bancroft, who was to succeed Whitgift at Canterbury, was well aware of the latent strength of the movement even though its noisier members had been suppressed. It was for the moment lacking in influential leaders because its friends in the Privy Council were dead, and with them the great Puritan peers such as Bedford, Warwick and Huntingdon. As President of the Council of the North, Huntingdon had fought the Catholics in their own stronghold by infiltrating godly ministers.

But these councillors and peers had done their work. Cambridge, where Burghley was chancellor, had bred a whole generation of students exposed to Puritan beliefs, and at Oxford Leicester had slowly undermined the contrary influences established in their brief opportunity by the Marian bishops. In the schools there were many earnest teachers like Thomas Beard, author of the ominously entitled *Theatre of God's Judgments*, who gave Cromwell his first instruction at the free school in Huntingdon. The Reformed worship was necessarily tolerated in the chapels of Dutch and Huguenot refugees, but it was practised also by the English merchant communities on the Continent, and the navy's ships were miniature Genevas. In much of the midlands, East Anglia and the south, the law of the Church was virtually disregarded. Corporations and wealthy patrons appointed, and often financed, ministers and lecturers who wore no vestments, gave their own meaning to the administration of the sacraments, and preached in churches stripped of their ornaments. In parishes where an ignorant or disaffected priest mumbled his way through the morning office, a bright young lecturer would appear in the afternoon to give the faithful the nourishment they needed. All this was done with the connivance or encouragement of the Justices of the Peace who were required to administer the statutory law. The long official struggle between Elizabeth and the Puritans tells only half the story. It was accompanied by the steady, unobtrusive penetration of lay opinion, and if, as is sometimes stated, Puritanism was 'driven underground' in the 1590s, it was because in London and many other important areas Puritan ways of thought and worship had quietly taken root.

The intellectual leader of the Puritans at the end of the reign was William Perkins, inevitably a Cambridge man, who had once belonged to a *classis* but was now steering them away from overmuch concern with matters of organisation. This was the first decade of Puritan scholasticism, and Perkins radiated, however deceptively, a mild reasonableness that reassured the lay supporters who had been temporarily alienated by the extravagances of the 1580s. Whereas Calvin said that only God could

31

know who was saved, Perkins peaceably held that it was known by all to whom the Gospel had been revealed. He taught a non-dogmatic Calvinism which stressed preaching, individual piety, Sabbath observance and the prayer and worship of the godly household. This was modest enough, and only the Sabbath was really a contentious issue. Calvin, it is true, played bowls on a Sunday, but the Puritans had been demanding that the day be exclusively set aside for worship, prayer and religious discussion. In *The Doctrine of the Sabbath* (1595) Dr Nicholas Bownde contended that strict Sabbath observance was the only part of the Jewish ritual that remained as a perpetual obligation. His arguments from Scripture and the early Fathers were, as in much else, debatable, but a reasonable Sunday observance, accepting works of necessity and mercy, was in the spirit of the Puritan conception of a godly society [8]. Catholic practices had been insufficiently reformed when men were still able to work before the service and indulge in sport and recreation after it, but there was also an element of economic rationalisation. By making Sunday the recognised day of rest, Sabbatarians proposed to abolish the numerous 'holy days' or feasts that, besides being pagan in themselves and a temptation to drunkenness and riot, kept labourers from the bench and plough. This was to become a surprisingly bitter controversy. Many doubted whether the law could intervene between the worker and his master, and in the *Book of Sports* (1618) James I insisted that healthy recreation prevented gossip, idleness and sedition, and fitted men for their military duties. A rigid Sunday observance would only win converts to the more indulgent attitude of Rome.

But there were graver disputes than this. In a momentous sermon at St Paul's in 1589 Bancroft challenged the Calvinist position by asserting that there was no scriptural basis for the Presbyterian system and that the superiority of bishops over other ministers was of divine ordination. Episcopacy existed *de iure divino*, and not just by permission of the monarch. Hooker, in the *Laws of Ecclesiastical Polity* (1594–7), said that episcopacy was sanctioned by the apostles but he would not allow that it was an indispensable necessity, since the government of a Church is that which the Church itself constitutes with divine authority to do so. In a detailed examination of Puritan arguments Hooker patiently evolved the essential Anglican position. Where God's prescription in Scripture was unmistakable and clear, it was to be obeyed. But different nations might require different institutions, and 'it is no more to the disgrace of Scripture to have left a number of other things free to be ordered at the discretion of the Church than for Nature to have left it unto the wit of man to devise his own attire'. There could be local variations without breach of our fundamental Christian unity, and the need to reform Catholic abuses had not separated us from 'the Church we were of before'. Where Scripture was silent, the Church might be guided by reason and tradition, 'the wisdom which is learned by tract of time', and Hooker appealed to the Puritans to restrain their zeal for an imagined perfection before it disrupted the peace and order of society [9].

This debate was still in the familiar area of ecclesiastical government. It was from sour, ungentle Cambridge that a challenge emerged also on doctrinal issues. In a Latin sermon delivered at Cambridge William Barret questioned the certainty of salvation and said that the first and proper cause of reprobation was sin. The Lambeth Articles repudiated such ideas, but the articles themselves were criticised by Peter Baro, a Frenchman holding Cartwright's old chair as Lady Margaret Professor. His arguments were similar to those of the Dutchman Arminius: that God created all men to eternal life, and Christ died for all; that each man is a self-determining agent and may embrace, reject or lose the salvation that is offered to him. In face of this terrible choice the usages and accumulated wisdom of the Church could help the worshipper to approach his God. Images and music stirred his reverence, the priest in the authority of his office broke down barriers, and man could without impiety use his aesthetic gifts to praise the Saviour from whom he received them.

Any supposed differences between Elizabethan and Stuart Puritanism may therefore be explained by the change in the nature of the conflict. The Church of England had stumbled unheroically through dangerous years. The mere fact of survival had dignified and enriched it, and it was evolving a positive identity that did not depend only on convenience and expediency and the Laodicean temper of the Queen. Calvinist doctrine and organisation were no longer the only necessary means to a godly life,

3

Politics and Trade

Puritanism was a genuinely religious movement, not a cloak for an ambitious *bourgeoisie*. But it was in its nature to make societies more difficult to govern, and its demands upon the magistrate, linked with an ecclesiastical discipline that threatened tithes and advowsons as well as episcopal estates, encouraged social and political change. In relatively sophisticated communities like France and England it was virtually proposing an alternative society.

It may have been only dimly realised at the time, but the Puritans' long contest with Elizabeth considerably strengthened Parliament in relation to the Crown. Henry VIII's supremacy in religion had been personal, even to the extent of allowing him to pronounce doctrine, and Parliament's role had been merely to sanction an arrangement not of its own making. But the Uniformity Acts of Edward VI and Elizabeth—respectively a minor and a female, and so thought to be incapable of exercising supremacy in their own persons—were specifically 'enacted by authority of Parliament'. The Puritans therefore had a case when they argued that the Commons might properly debate and alter a Prayer Book whose use had been prescribed by statute. Against this, Elizabeth insisted that all religious matters lay within the prerogative whose powers she had delegated to the officers of the Church and the ecclesiastical commissions, and she refused to allow them to be discussed in Parliament. She succeeded, more or less, but in these disputes the Commons were able to extend and consolidate their privileges and procedure. Peter Wentworth knew what he was about. Forbidden to discuss religion, he shifted his ground to the issue of privilege, protesting against the Crown's interference in the Commons' lawful proceedings and asserting that the right to freedom of speech included the right to initiate matters for discussion. The organised Puritan group in Parliament was probably quite small, but it caused the Commons to become increasingly conscious of their powers, and the pressure came from other points besides the efforts to alter the Prayer Book and Church government. The Queen's childlessness, a manifest sign of God's displeasure with a sinful nation, led to disputes about marriage and the succession, as Protestantism had a vested interest in the continuance of the Tudor line. The Commons harassed the government about Mary Queen of Scots, and finally won their point, and they were always urging an aggressive foreign policy on behalf of the Huguenots and the Dutch. This would incidentally include the capture of overseas territories as a means of annoying Spain, making commercial profits and converting the heathen savage [10]. The Crown, which had led the nation in the early stages of the Reformation, was now everywhere on the defensive, and in her tenderness for the prerogative Elizabeth had to abandon bills she wanted Parliament to pass, and refuse to call it when her financial needs were pressing.

This was the crux. The dominating issue of the sixteenth century, as important politically as in social and economic life, was inflation, which undermined the traditional powers of the Crown, the Church and the aristocracy. Because of the price-rise the 'Tudor despotism' was potentially dangerous only during the brief windfall of the monastery lands, and two-thirds of these had been disposed of by 1547. A poll tax, literally a capital levy, had been attempted in 1512, and Wolsey, whose efforts as a financier have not been given their due, experimented with a graduated income-tax based on a realistic assessment of taxpayers' wealth. But these devices were not repeated, and the futile wars of the 1540s meant that bankruptcy was averted only by debasement and a fresh wave of ecclesiastical plunder. The foreign mercenaries who had helped to suppress the risings of 1549 had to be paid off and thereafter the Tudor monarchy lacked the essential sinews of despotism, money, bureaucracy, and a standing army.

Elizabeth's early wars in Scotland and France cost £750,000 and her 'ordinary' revenue from Customs, Crown dues and property was about £200,000 a year, rising to £300,000 by the end of the reign. Through revenue from the Customs she could take her share of the increasing profits of trade, but this was the Crown's only means of keeping pace with inflation. It is little wonder that the Queen kept out of war when she could. Aid to the Netherlands cost £130,000 a year, and military expenditure after 1589 amounted to three million pounds.

Taxation granted by Parliament consisted of the old tenths and fifteenths, fixed at £30,000, and the subsidy, supposed to yield £100,000 but declining to £80,000. As the value of money fell, Parliament had to be

35

asked for two or three subsidies instead of one, which made them feel they were paying bigger taxes than they actually were. Assessments were made by the JPs and so were unrealistic, and the collection was mostly left to 'tax-farmers' who were unpopular and dishonest. This taxation was regarded as 'extraordinary' revenue granted for particular purposes, and in order to get it the Queen had to expose herself to wrangles about privilege, religion and other matters of concern to the Commons, who increasingly tended to discuss their grievances before they would vote supply. To avoid this steady erosion of the prerogative she had to find other sources of revenue. Improved administration in the 1590s increased the yield of the feudal dues, notably wardship and purveyance, but this led to complaints against these survivals of a superannuated system. Elizabeth I sold Crown lands worth an average of £20,000 a year throughout the reign, which was living off capital, and she sold tithes in more than two thousand parishes, the loss of the advowsons weakening her control of clerical appointments. It should now be clear why she also kept bishoprics vacant, exploited clerical first-fruits and made the bishops surrender their lands to courtiers and officials who would otherwise have received no salaries. It has been estimated that the cost of providing an efficient bureaucracy would have been £600,000 a year. As this money did not exist, royal servants had to be rewarded in other ways, or allowed to take their own percentage from the perquisites of office. From a high-minded view—such as the parliamentary and Puritan opposition habitu-ally took—there was corruption in every branch of the public adminis-tration. It was unavoidable. The only cure was to provide the Crown with an adequate income through the overhaul of a fiscal system that was hopelessly antiquated even before inflation had made it worse. In this reign and the next the Cecils proposed some tentative reforms, but these efforts would always break down on Parliament's reluctance to agree to a regular income that might enable the Crown to govern independently.

The imminent collapse of the system was apparent in the quarrel about monopolies in the last two parliaments of the reign. Within the Crown's acknowledged duty to regulate trade in the national interest, the grant of a monopoly rewarded initiative and encouraged investment. But under the pressure of inflation it simply became another way of rewarding cour tiers and royal servants, and monopolies came to embrace such an enor-mous range of goods and services that they were a sort of value-added tax on every kind of consumer activity and so were themselves inflation-ary. The superb felicity with which Elizabeth conducted her retreat in 1601 could not conceal a vital shift in the balance of power. She knew it herself, because she immediately forestalled another likely attack by commanding an audit of the administration of purveyance. Parliamentary taxation in the last fifteen years of her reign was three times the total of the previous thirty years, and in the Crown's continuing necessity the Commons could make their grants conditional upon the satisfaction of their own demands. They were certain, therefore, to resist any attempt to increase the Crown's revenue from non-parliamentary sources. With this there was a growing opposition to the Crown's independent jurisdiction in the prerogative courts. Star Chamber and the other conciliar courts were still popular for their relatively swift and inexpensive procedure, but although the Reformation had removed the authority of Rome, canon law was still the basis of the law administered in the ecclesiastical courts. These courts were everywhere disliked, and not only by the common lawyers who suffered financially. They were controlled by the bishops, which in itself was an offence to the Puritans, and as well as dealing with heresy, probate and matrimonial affairs, they enforced the collection of tithes and other lay payments to the clergy and they still exercised the Church's traditional authority over morals. They were accused of imposing the dread sentence of excommunication for trivial offences and of being more interested in the extraction of fines and fees than in a true concern for the moral welfare of the people. Theirs was a debased form of the ecclesiastical discipline demanded by the Puritans. Opposition was concentrated by Whitgift's use of High Commission for the political purpose of suppressing nonconformity, and it would be directed eventually at the other conciliar courts as well. Already writs of prohibition were being issued to bring particular cases to the courts of common law. A demand for a single uniform administration of the law was a counter to courts where important policy-making decisions might be given in the guise of judicial verdicts.

In 1593 James Morice, attorney of the Court of Wards, was sent to the Tower for introducing bills for the reform of the ecclesiastical courts, but he was speaking as a lawyer as well as a Puritan and he was claiming for the Commons a right to proceed by statute against any defects in the royal administration. It was all very well for Elizabeth to tell the Commons, in the same year, that their liberty of speech consisted in saying yea or nay to bills. Her techniques of parliamentary management were wearing thin with the loss of councillors such as Mildmay and Knollys, who were on good terms with the Puritan backbenchers, and the Commons were learning how to sidestep royal control of the sessions by going into committee or constituting themselves as a Committee of the Whole House for which the Speaker would not be in the chair. The Queen had to rely increasingly on proclamations and other forms of non-statutory regulation, and over-use weakened the instruments—particularly the bishops—on which she depended. Her habitual scolding lost its force on a body with which she now had to contend on more equal terms. In the sixteenth century the Commons increased their membership from 296 to 462, mainly through pressure from the landed gentry who were willing to put up with expense and inconvenience in their desire to be represented. Having created sixty-two new borough seats by 1586, Elizabeth at length got the message and granted no more charters for the representation of independently-minded country gentlemen likely to be Puritan in sympathy and mistrustful of many of the policies of the court.

While the Crown and the Church were becoming politically and financially weaker, many sections of the population were growing wealthier and seeking the political influence that goes with money, land and social position. In recent years historians have tried to measure the importance in the English Revolution of a declining, or alternatively rising, gentry. There is no space to discuss their arguments here, and possibly the debate has been a shade too academic. The reader may find an admirably objective account of it by Professor Stone, one of the more vigorous participants, in his *The Causes of the English Revolution* (pages 26–40). The value of this debate, whatever conclusions may be extracted from it, is that it has drawn attention to the extraordinary social upheaval of the period.

In the sixteenth century the population rose from $2\frac{1}{2}$ to 4 millions, and possibly about a third of the land changed hands. Estates were acquired by merchants, lawyers and investors who not only formed a new landed class but brought a new attitude to ownership by exploiting their property through improved agricultural methods and the development of mineral resources. Copyholders were forced out by prohibitive increases in rent when their leases fell in, and land, hitherto the basis of all social and political relationships, came under the laws of a market economy. Enclosure improved the agricultural yield as well as favouring sheep-farming, and progressive Tudor landlords experimented with techniques usually associated with eighteenth-century improving farmers such as 'Turnip' Townshend and Coke of Holkham. Consequently the laws against enclosure were resented as a restriction on capital investment in land, and in 1593 they were repealed. Four years later, a series of rain-ruined harvests led to a new Tillage Act, but this was an emergency measure that was soon swept aside. Stock-breeding, crop rotation and the reclaiming of fens and marshes bore witness to an immense energy that in some areas transformed the old subsistence economy based on the stable village community. The new race of wealthy sheep-masters and graziers also wanted to put their profits into industry, and there was small-scale capitalism in the cloth and coal trades especially, with efforts to encourage the 'finishing' of textiles in England instead of shipping the raw material to continental centres. Industries were started, often with the help of Protestant refugees, in small towns free of the close regulation imposed in older cities by the mediaeval guilds. This economic initiative is to be found again in the readiness to subscribe to naval expeditions in search of new markets overseas, and here the 'interlopers', as the new speculators were called, challenged the established trading companies such as the Merchant Adventurers, and the Eastland, the Muscovy and the Levant Companies. These corporations paid substantial fees to the Crown for exclusive trading rights in certain areas, and they were naturally jealous of their monopoly. The interlopers did not see why they should not break into this lucrative trade, and in particular there was widespread resentment of the wealth and commercial privileges of the City of London. A free trade bill in the Commons in 1604 was eventually dropped, but the debate illustrated the unpopularity of all these commercial restrictions [11].

In the remote and backward parts of the country this economic change was hardly noticed, but there is no doubt that, in general, it produced a vigorous class of men who had found a way to beat inflation and had little sympathy for its victims. The victims included many of the aristocracy, who had to sell their estates to avoid bankruptcy. Some families realised in time the importance of administering their lands efficiently, and they tended to form marriage alliances with the new commercial families whose methods they had learned to imitate. But by 1600 the Lords had lost much of their wealth and influence in relation to the Commons. In the country at large these changes in the social balance led to some anxiety about the disappearance of old landmarks and the overturning of 'degree'. In his *Description of England* (1577) William Harrison, an Anglican parson, is a valuable witness because, although he is proud and patriotic and wants to think the best of his people, he cannot help deploring the wealth, the imported fashions and the social restlessness of a generation he does not fully understand. The Elizabethan dramatists, whose conservative affection for the old ways and institutions is often overlooked, expressed a similar point of view. Chapman, Marston and Jonson were fierce against the entrepreneurs and 'projectors', while Heywood and Dekker presented an idealised picture of a simpler and happier London life. In Shakespeare's *Twelfth Night* Malvolio was not 'consanguineous' as Sir Toby was, and he was a social upstart expecting to achieve greatness or have it thrust upon him. (Or by 'greatness' was Shakespeare, at a safe remove from explicit religious controversy, really thinking of 'grace'?)

In economic affairs, as in religion, the Crown was attached to a policy no longer apt for the times. The intention was worthy enough: a traditional paternalism that should protect the weak from the strong, maintain the quality of goods, keep both wages and prices at an equitable level and regulate the economy in the general interest of the nation. But under Queen Elizabeth, and still more under the Stuarts, this policy presented itself as an enervating conservatism that hampered economic progress.

Governments have a natural interest in preserving the social structure, and the Crown was not exclusively concerned with profits and the maximum utilisation of resources. The Statute of Artificers (1563), with its rigid code for apprenticeship, was designed to restrict the use of casual labour. On the other hand, social mobility was necessary for the diversification and expansion of trade, especially in the industries being established in non-incorporated towns. The Crown tried to restrict enclosure, which was thought to be depopulating the rural areas, but enclosure could grow more food, save the importing of corn and make it profitable to cultivate the less fertile land. The Crown tried to maintain wages and employment even during bad harvests and trade recessions, but in practice JPs obeyed market conditions and supplemented wages from the poor-rate levied on the parish. The Crown wanted to supervise internal trade and standards of workmanship through the guilds; overseas, in order to protect the privileged companies which concentrated on certain markets, the Crown maintained envoys in the countries where they traded and organised convoys to guard their shipping. But this policy was often ineffective against foreign competition, and it hindered the development of growing industries such as the 'new draperies', lighter cloths for which there was an increasing demand. Again, a foreign policy undertaken for non-economic motives might conflict with certain economic interests. Sir Edward Coke would maintain that 'England never throve so well as when at war with Spain', and this was to be the general view of Stuart Parliaments. In fact it is impossible to say that there was a common 'merchant interest' in foreign policy since different trades had different objectives and there were companies which benefited when there was peace with Spain and they could develop their competition with the Dutch. But at all times there were particular pressures on the government to pursue a foreign policy that favoured a sectional economic interest.

At best, therefore, royal paternalism hindered industrial advance and

channelled much capital investment into non-productive a
machinery of enforcement was clumsy and ultimately unenl
because there was no bureaucracy to make it work and the JPs
not prosecute breaches of the law where their own advantage wa
volved. The interlopers took to 'piracy' in defiance of the privileged companies, and the Earl of Warwick, who brought the navy on to Parliament's side in the Civil War, had many years of successful piracy behind
him. The Crown, too, had mercenary considerations of its own. Certain
trades were encouraged because they brought revenue through the Customs, and monopolies, which were supposed to encourage enterprise,
were a form of unofficial taxation which inflated prices, limited output
and failed to protect the consumer.

It would be wrong to suggest that Puritanism had any conscious economic theory, and its identification with the growth of *bourgeois* capitalism has been exaggerated, but here, as in politics, its essential character was impatient of restriction and gave an impetus to free individual
expression. The Puritan was certainly more interested in shops than in
crops, but he worked not in order to achieve salvation but in order to be
assured of it. To avoid the stigma of idleness and dissipation, he dedicated himself to gainful labour and did not stop when he had made
enough. It is true that this is an indispensable element of capitalism,
which deals in surpluses and is not content with the satisfaction of immediate and local needs, but to the Puritan, economic activity was not so
much an end in itself as a sign of an upright character and a zeal to promote God's kingdom by the suppression of idleness and vice. This helped
to stimulate the expansionist energy of the age and was in conflict with
the anachronistic economic policies of the Crown.

4

Art and Morals

*O infinite virtue, comest thou smiling from
The world's great snare uncaught?*
ANTONY AND CLEOPATRA IV viii 17

When asked 'What is the world?' Cromwell replied, 'All that cools my
love for the Saviour.' Many Puritans were cultivated men: Cromwell
himself enjoyed music, dancing and pastoral at his court, Milton the
scrivener spent hours with his son among books, madrigals and foreign
studies, Mrs Hutchinson says that her husband delighted in fencing,
music and all the liberal arts, Fairfax forbade his troopers to sack the
Bodleian Library, and so on. Learned men studied the Bible and early
Christian writings to produce an orderly arrangement of doctrine, and
the stimulus was not only intellectual. Deeper feelings were stirred by
the contemplation of the awful mysteries of sin, God's covenant with
man and redemption through Christ's redeeming grace. All this is far
removed from the extravagances of the lunatic fringe, the ravings of
men like Gosson and Northbrooke against the theatre, or of Philip
Stubbes against football, maypoles, fashion, May games, Whitsun ales,
the use of starch and the 'whoredoms and filthy Sodomitical exercises' of
anyone he disliked [12]. In the early days this sort of thing was not typical; and possibly it was not typical of the movement as a whole even
when in the middle of the seventeenth century the victorious sects, urged
on by their preachers, let loose a flood of inhibitions.

But the sober Puritan was always mindful of the warning of earlier
Churches that had abused God's gifts. Richard Baxter discovered a 'universal and radical enmity between ... the serpent and the woman's seed,
the fleshly mind and the spiritual law of God'. A Christian's duty was to
surrender to God's omnipotence, not to try to understand him through
the intellect or worship him through the senses. Carlstadt (né Boden-
stein), a disciple whom Luther hastened to reject, had denounced aesthetic pleasure as a seduction prompted by man's carnal imagination,

and Jeremy Collier, a later Puritan who attacked the Restoration stage, was only putting this in an extreme form when he said that 'music is almost as dangerous as gunpowder'.

So we have the paradox of men who were not themselves uncivilised taking up an attitude that in the long run was hostile to culture. They were not just following Sir Nathaniel's advice in *Love's Labour's Lost* to 'abrogate scurrility'. The Puritans' mistrust of artistic expression went far beyond the moral discipline necessary to godly living, and the explanation was their hatred and fear of Rome. Catholic worship made use of sensuous aids which, for the Puritans, elevated the priest and came between the believer and his God. Their revulsion took the form of an emotional iconoclasm which made 'bare ruin'd choirs where late the sweet birds sang'. Images were defaced, shrines defiled, pictures and ornaments despoiled, and there was a good deal of symbolic urinating in fonts. Marston's Malcontent had seen 'a sumptuous steeple turned to a stinking privy: more beastly, the sacredest place made a dog's kennel: nay, most inhuman, the ston'd coffins of long-fled Christians burst up and made hogs' troughs'. Even Fairfax despoiled the 'malignant cathedral' of Canterbury which to Erasmus had been 'so eminent that it puts religion into a man's thoughts as far as he can see it'.

Disgust with Roman ceremonial largely accounts for Puritan opposition to the drama. There were other reasons too: the theatres encouraged cozening, immorality and riot, they helped to spread the plague and they attracted audiences that might otherwise have been listening to sermons. Almost every age has produced men of high sensibility, like Plato, who have thought drama to be dangerous because *mimesis* forces the actor into characters that are not his own, but the Puritan objection was to its origin in the ritual of the mediaeval Church, 'when the great scarlet-coloured whore of Babylon . . . set the church door wide open for sundry sports and plays to enter freely into the house of God'. Plays, said Stubbes, were 'sucked out of the devil's teats to nourish us in idolatry, heathenry and sin'. In London, Puritan influence in the City corporation was so strong that the players had to move their theatres outside the walls, and the dramatists naturally responded by deriding the men who imperilled their livelihood. Hypocrisy, or self-deception, was the principal charge: the sacred invocations and professions of godliness, and the difference between the profession and the act. It exasperated ordinary men when the Puritan tediously referred every action to his conscience. Shakespeare's Sir Nathaniel smugly approved the royal stag-hunt as 'very reverend sport, truly, and done in the testimony of a good conscience'. This is a palpable hit. Eating pig on a feast day might be idolatrous, but Zeal-of-the-Land Busy in Ben Jonson's *Bartholomew Fair* pronounces absolution: 'We may be religious in the midst of the profane, so it be eaten with a reformed mouth'. He seizes the toys from a stall at the fair because they are superstitious relics, and he rebukes the gingerbread-seller for 'thy basket of Popery, thy nest of images'. Widow Purecraft permits her daughter (called Win-the-Fight Littlewit) to gaze enthralled at the fair's attractions so long as she hates them 'as our brother Zeal does'.

The dramatists had their fun, and with reservations it is useful evidence, but the Puritans wore them down. An Act in 1606 to prohibit profanity on the stage had the curious result of causing Malvolio, in the only surviving text, to invoke the pagan Jove instead of the jealous deity he clearly had in mind, but this was only a minor irritant. The Puritan attacks subsided when Elizabeth and James I were evidently determined to have their plays at court, but they were once again thunderous when Charles I married a drama-loving Catholic queen and the Arminian clergy revived ceremonial in the churches. William Prynne's *Histriomastix* (1632) brought out the old arguments about the 'transvestites' who played the women's parts, and because all Puritans believed that the priest at the Mass was 'acting Christ', they said that drama was tainted at the source. Plays were also evil because they were accompanied by 'lust-provoking music' and 'amorous dancing'. Prynne was a thoroughgoing Biblical literalist (although Aubrey complained of his 'unfaithful quotations') and he employed typical casuistry in his interpretation of the text. David's dancing was 'innocent of gropings' and Solomon's merely denoted 'an inward cheerfulness'. Plays were also said to provoke unhallowed laughter, since Scripture only tells us that Jesus wept. The whole scriptural thesis against the drama is absurdly unhistorical since the early Christians were condemning the deliberately salacious orgies of a pagan society, and that is no good reason for supposing that they would have condemned a fundamentally serious drama that originated in church. But the effect was to deprive the Puritans of a popular medium which they might have used most successfully for their own purposes. They had an exemplum in Bishop Bale's *King Johan* (c. 1536), a remarkable essay in psychopathic Protestantism which, leaving out inconvenient episodes like Magna Carta, presented John as the morning star of the Reformation against the imperialism of the Roman Antichrist. It is possible to contemplate, although fortunately it did not happen, a whole corpus of didactic drama compiled by earnest Puritan clergymen.

In 1642 the theatres were closed, but the damage had been done before that. It is true that the new vogue of the indoor theatre, with its more exclusive audience, cut off the drama from its popular roots, but it was the intellectuals who failed. The Jacobeans retreated into melodrama and spurious romantic comedy. A single example is Beaumont and Fletcher's *Philaster* (1611), where a young prince is in Hamlet's predicament: he is told by the usurping king to be better-tempered, 'the bravery of his mind' is admired by the populace who are in arms on his behalf, he is possessed by his dead father's spirit and reminded that he is a king, and is suspected by the court of mental derangement. In the outcome he solves his problems by marrying the usurper's daughter. This appalling levity is characteristic of a drama which might raise great issues but would smother them in the end in the mechanical contrivances of the plot. In spite of the incidental pleasures and excitements, the impression is of sensationalism and sentimentality and a refusal to attempt, as all art should, 'a criticism of life'. This is perhaps a tribute to the devastating finality of Puritan thought, which on large matters had left so little more to be said. It can only be loss when the intellect has to be satisfied with a methodological exposition of the great mysteries, human and divine, and is thought to be too weak to be allowed to explain them. Puritanism had an abundant literature of precept hammered home by scholarly precedents, but it had no intellectual foundations. Nor was it vitalised by imagination, because imagination was carnal and fed the passions. Spenser's innate poetic gift was compromised by a year he spent at Cartwright's feet at Cambridge. As though wary of poetry as a lawful exercise, he had to moralise romance and introduce extraneous dogma. Milton was a Humanist never afraid to use classical models, but *Paradise Lost* has pages of doctrinaire theology unsuitable for epic. He was the least mystical of all great poets, and *Paradise Lost* contains less mysticism than the pagan *Aeneid*.

Forbidden to explore the unknowable, the questing intellect turned quite congenially to more practical matters, and there was some excellent writing on economic theory and science, topics, in the well-worn phrase, dissociated from sensibility. This was to the advantage of both literature and science, but it was no part of the Puritan intention that God's universe should be studied other than through God's personal revelation. In a different vein there was Caroline poetry, light and short-lived as gossamer, or the intellectual complexities of the Anglican preachers, who seemed to be using words as an escape from reality. Aubrey tells of a Scottish lord who remarked of Bishop Lancelot Andrewes that 'he was learned, but he did play with his text as a Jack-an-apes does, who takes up a thing and tosses and plays with it, and then he takes up another and plays a little with it. Here's a pretty thing, and there's a pretty thing!'

After 1611, the year of the Authorised Version and Shakespeare's withdrawal from the theatre, there is a sudden death of the art that instantly explains and satisfies.

Music also suffered from the Puritans' dislike of Catholic ritual. They complained to Convocation of worship that was 'abused by piping of organs; singing, ringing and trowling of psalms from one side to another; with the squeaking of chanting choristers'. Singing in church must be congregational, and not staged for theatrical effect by choristers maintained for no other purpose. This sounds simple, but it needed a different kind of music. Instead of the polyphonic music of the cathedrals, the Puritans used 'Sternhold and Hopkins', a rhyming psalter set to ballad tunes like *Chevy Chase*. As hymns were inadmissible as unscriptural, these 'Genevan jigs' came to be very important, and in time the creeds and canticles received the same treatment. Thus parts of the liturgy were debased to doggerel and sung to popular accompaniments, to the great discouragement of serious organists and musicians. When in the 1640s the Puritans closed the cathedrals, they dispersed the choirs and musicians, who were never restored to their former state. Charles II introduced the fiddle from France, and from that time the great bulk of 'English' music has been imported. This is difficult to explain. It is much too strange a thing to be attributed solely to Puritanism or any other isolated cause.

In painting the position may seem to be different, as James I and Prince Henry were enthusiastic collectors and Charles I was the most distinguished royal patron of art this country has known. He employed the Dutch artist Daniel Mytens as king's painter and Inigo Jones as surveyor of works; he brought Van Dyck to England, and although he could not persuade Rubens to stay as well, he gave him numerous commissions. Charles discovered Titian during the disastrous visit to Spain in 1623, and in 1628 he bought the Duke of Mantua's collection with money voted for a naval expedition. The drawback to this brief cultural flowering was that so few people took part in it or had the taste and knowledge to appreciate it. Court masques, Palladian architecture and the portraiture of Van Dyck were essentially aristocratic things, and to the country at large a source of alienation. Puritans saw only the luxury and extravagance, 'Nonesuch Charles squandering away millions of pounds on braveries and vanities, on old rotten pictures and broken-nosed marbles'. A taste for paintings only confirmed their suspicion that Charles was flirting with Popery, and on his death almost the whole of his incomparable collection was dispersed on the international market.

By 1640 there were two cultures in England, with Humanist culture eroded by the Puritans' high ethical seriousness and hatred of anything Roman. If art was not actually immoral, it had sensuous dangers that could easily make it so, and Prynne was sure that it was one of the devices the Jesuits used to seduce the Indian native. In this issue, as in so much else, the Crown and the hierarchy were on the losing side.

The Crown failed to keep pace with inflation, and its success in containing the Puritans, Spain and the Counter-Reformation was won at a high cost in wealth and influence. James I's inherited debt of £400,000— more than a year's revenue—was only a small external token of his real legacy. Thus it would be quite convincing to explain the seventeenth-century revolution in simple Marxist terms, and in *Oceana* (1656) James Harrington did suggest something of the kind. Short of a drastic fiscal reconstruction that the parliamentary gentry would never permit, the propertied classes had to have a greater share in government and from there it was not a long step to the sovereignty of Parliament.

But Marxist explanations ignore the accidental and the personal, and even economically inevitable revolutions require a driving-force. It would seem that in England this dynamic was supplied by Puritanism, a creed which was active rather than contemplative and knew that it had to overcome secular obstacles before God's kingdom could be established. It sanctified resistance to the magistrate if he were corrupt, and it would not be detained by 'the puddles of history', by which it meant privilege, prerogative and tradition. Eventually it would succumb to its inherent contradiction between the sovereignty of the individual conscience and the need for an ordered society. When Cromwell appealed 'to the natural magistracy of the nation', he was saying that the godly community could only be established by men of substance. But the Puritans were fierce, uncompromising opponents. They would wrestle with Antichrist in all his shapes, and even to their own terrible God they would not genuflect. 'Blessed is he that dasheth the brats of Babylon against the stones', said Hanserd Knollys, a Puritan preacher, in 1641. Their demand for spiritual reform and a learned preaching ministry awakened a vital response in Elizabethan England and accounts for the widespread support given by a laity with varied and sometimes conflicting objectives. Lawyers, projectors, constitutionalists, merchants, social visionaries, seamen, magistrates: the people of God had something to offer to all these, and had a dedicated energy that promised to lead them to their various destinations.

47

1

Breakdown

O polish'd perturbation! golden care!
2 HENRY IV IV v 23

James I was a lazy intellectual who drank too much. He may have had other vices too, and by skilful propaganda Puritan morality managed in this reign to drive a wedge between court and nation. Mrs Hutchinson, who was not born until 1620, was brought up in the belief that James's court was 'a nursery of lust and intemperance' so infective that every great house under its influence became 'a sty of uncleanness'. The opposition exaggerated, but undoubtedly there was a swinishness, notably Somerset's marriage to the divorced Countess of Essex and the subsequent murder of Overbury. These messy affairs widened a gap that was already becoming conscious and explicit. James cheapened the nobility by doubling the lay peerage, with titles fetching as much as £10,000, and he sold so many baronetcies, a rank created by himself, that the price dropped in the market from £1,095 to little more than £200. Uncouth favourites from Scotland competed for the indiscriminate distribution of lands, jewels and heiresses, and the Puritans observed with mistrust the tangible marks of favour granted to bishops and chaplains who toed the official line. This squalid traffic in rewards and offices went far beyond the recognised need to provide a livelihood for public servants or regulate the economy. It was given fresh momentum with the ascendancy of Buckingham, exalted, according to the ever-charitable Mrs Hutchinson, 'upon no merit but his beauty and prostitution'. Actually he was brought to James's notice, with possets and other medications to improve his midlands complexion, by a group that included George Abbot, the Calvinist Archbishop of Canterbury, with the object of supplanting the Catholic Howards. Once arrived, he exploited a reckless patronage that Queen Elizabeth had carefully withheld from Leicester and Essex, and the Crown was diminished in prestige when not only the hereditary peers but able and ambitious men like Bacon and Coke had to grovel to the upstart for their share in the bonanza.

On the question of Divine Right James I was much less absurd than is usually supposed. Divine Right was the ultimate sanction of degree, the family and a patriarchal order of society. Few Elizabethans would have challenged the mystical conception of kingship that Shakespeare put into the mouth of Richard II, and it was in this spirit that the poets gave thanks for Gloriana. 'It is a very fit similitude', James told Parliament in 1624, 'for a king and his people to be like to a husband and wife, for even as Christ, in whose throne I sit in this part of the earth, is husband to the Church, and the Church is His spouse, so I likewise desire to be your husband, and ye should be my spouse.' But Elizabeth had also told them that 'every one of you, and as many as are Englishmen, are children and kinsmen to me', and James was only expressing in his over-rhetorical way what had implicitly been the Tudor attitude. He even had a special reason for this, since he acquired a Messianic aura by his safe appearance in England after the long years of doubt about the succession. His opening speech to Parliament in 1604, couched in richly figurative language, was printed and circulated to nourish a nation-wide expectation that the new reign, with the blessed union of the two thrones, would fulfil the ancient prophecies for which Henry VII had given the name Arthur to his eldest son. This Messianic devotion was renewed after James's miraculous deliverance from the Gunpowder Plot, a crime felt to be so incredible and outrageous that it explains his overwrought utterances about the blasphemy of resisting the Lord's anointed.

So too Shakespeare's Fleance was delivered from the crimes of Macbeth and was spared to lead his country out of darkness. James's address to Parliament in 1610 shows that he did not interpret Divine Right as a permission to violate fundamental law [13], and although he sometimes took short cuts, as in the use of letters patent to affirm the authority of High Commission in 1611, he seldom exceeded his prerogative as the law and practice of the constitution then defined it. Even his habit of supposedly trying to influence the judges was not really improper, since judicial verdicts were often the first essential step in giving force to policy. Although Coke is believed to have attempted to move in this direction, English judges do not pronounce upon the justice and morality of the law they administer. Their duty is to enforce what they consider to be the government's intention as expressed in statutes, orders and proclamations, and it is not necessary to see in James's so-called interference anything more sinister than an attempt to explain this intention in particular cases. His real mistake was to protest too much about his authority and rights. The Commons were not disposed to act just as a backdrop for Solomon, and he was too fond of telling them that 'we are an old and experienced King' who proposed to be 'the great schoolmaster of the whole land'. Like Ethelred, he was 'unready': meaning that he would not seek or listen to advice because he already knew all that he needed to know. But when he insisted on defining the mysteries which he forbade his subjects to invade, the loftiness of the theory looked faintly ridiculous beside the continued failure in action. The reign went wrong from the start, as, with the difficulties of James's inheritance, it probably had to. A series of separate disputes, about religion, privilege, finance, trading rights, the sources and administration of the law, gradually fused until they exploded into a constitutional crisis.

The trouble began with the Puritans, whose Millenary Petition (1603) requested Sabbath observance, a reduction in ceremonial, better stipends and the reform of plurality and other abuses. Excommunication was not to be pronounced 'under the name of lay persons, chancellors, officials, etc.' but only by consent of the pastor. These were the demands which the moderates had been making for years, and at Hampton Court James agreed to minor changes in the Prayer Book and to measures to improve the income from tithe. But he would not accept any changes in ritual or Church government, and he spluttered like a turkey-cock when someone mentioned presbytery. James, like Elizabeth, has been criticised for not going further to meet the Puritans' not unreasonable demands, but it is impossible to know what might have followed from even the slightest concessions. Although the petitioners denied that they were 'factious men affecting a popular parity', they were busy circulating a document recommending a discipline similar to that used in other Reformed Churches. In the Form of Apology and Satisfaction (1604), a protest document which probably never reached the King, the Commons meekly said that they did not come 'in any Puritan or Brownish spirit' in asking for 'the relinquishment of some few ceremonies of small importance'. It sounds innocent enough, but in the same paragraph they claimed that the Crown had no power 'either to alter religion . . or to make any laws concerning the same, otherwise than, as in temporal causes, by consent of Parliament'.

Bancroft, who succeeded Whitgift at Canterbury in 1604, had no illusions about the seeming mildness of the Puritan approach, and under his direction Convocation drafted fresh canons for the government of the Church. So far from making any concessions, these required all candidates for ordination not merely to subscribe to Whitgift's three articles but to subscribe 'willingly and *ex animo*', to swear, that is, that when they subscribed they meant what they said. James, who had already rebuked the Commons for introducing on their own initiative bills for religious reform, ordered the whole body of the clergy to conform to the established forms of worship; 'What intractable men do not perform upon admonition, they must be compelled unto by authority'. Petitions came in from all over the country, but about ninety recalcitrant clergy were ejected from their livings and some sixty more were suspended.

Religious grievances in one form or another were put forward in every parliamentary session up till 1629, and they were concerned not merely with worship and discipline but with the extent of the royal supremacy. The Commons, backed by the lawyers, questioned the right of Convocation to legislate for the Church without statutory backing, and the deprivation of ministers raised the old question of freehold. High Commission was again under fire, partly because it was an instrument of an unpopular policy and partly because the judges, led by Coke, were challenging all the courts that lay outside the common law, including Chancery, Requests and the commercial jurisdiction of the Admiralty. Writs of prohibition were issued to bring cases before the common law, and in this way many cases concerning tithe, heresy and clerical fees were withdrawn from High Commission and the ecclesiastical courts. Coke eventually over-reached himself and his colleagues were more cautious after his dismissal (1616), but fundamental issues were in dispute. Parliament and the judges had denied, in spite of earlier decisions under Elizabeth, that the Crown could set up a new court by means of a royal commission. Only Parliament could do this, and only the common law could interpret Parliament's decisions. In part these claims were due to dissatisfaction with the Crown's recourse to competing jurisdictions, as certainty should be the essence of the law. But the legal quarrel was being absorbed into the larger conflict, and it was mistrust of the Crown's religious policy that brought it to a head.

This mistrust hindered Bancroft's genuine attempts to reform the administration of the Church. So far as circumstances allowed, he was a great reforming bishop, but although he had not been the first to proclaim it, the Puritans would not accept his argument that episcopacy was an apostolic institution, and so they obstructed his efforts to bring about many of the improvements they had themselves demanded. After the panic of 1605 his success in reaching a pragmatic agreement with the Catholics was a further ground for suspicion, and he had little hope of winning support for his reforming plans. The real trouble, he said, was not that the bishops exercised too much jurisdiction but that their coercive power was insufficient to enable them to instruct and discipline the torpid and ignorant among the clergy. He reorganised the system of episcopal visitation, but this was not enough. Secondly, he tried to tackle the problem of inadequate incomes. Through the commutation of tithe into cash arrangements, nearly a third of the benefices were worth £5 a year or less, and very few were worth more than £25. These sums, originally for the support of a celibate clergy, had been overtaken by inflation and were now supposed to be sufficient for family men of the superior qualifications which the Puritans expected in the ministry. The Church was demanding better men for less money, but when Bancroft made proposals for the payment of tithes in kind, to represent a sensible economic value, he was defeated in the Commons by the gentry, many of whom were lay impropriators, and by the lawyers when he tried to contest titles in the ecclesiastical courts. The Commons' petition on religion in July 1610 asked for the recusancy laws to be enforced and the 'silenced brethren' to be restored, and complained that pluralism and non-residence left the people 'a prey to the Popish seducers'. It was a wholly negative document, and the real objective was revealed in a general petition on grievances in the same month, where in an attack on High Commission the Commons said that the Act of Supremacy itself was 'of dangerous extent in divers respects'.

Abbot, who succeeded Bancroft as Archbishop of Canterbury in 1611, was an unlikely appointment since he was known to be a rigid Calvinist who regarded bishops as superintendent pastors not essentially superior to any other order. But he had written fulsomely of James as 'undefiled as Jehosaphat or Hezekias', and his brother Maurice was a prominent trader in the City, an original member of the East India Company and an enthusiast for colonial settlements. Edward Hyde (later the Earl of Clarendon) said that Abbot's only criterion of a Christian religion was that it should abhor Popery, and he was strangely indifferent to the state of the parish clergy. But he was not a ritualist, and as he did not vex the clergy with religious tests the Puritans were comparatively quiet until the Thirty Years War and the spread of Arminianism revived the old cry of 'Protestantism in danger'.

James meanwhile was having other troubles. His first Parliament opened with a dispute about privilege in which the Commons established their right, as against Chancery, to be judges of disputed elections. In effect they had already achieved this under Elizabeth, but James had chosen to fight, with much high-flown language, and had been defeated. His peace with Spain in 1604 was unpopular with merchants whom it debarred from the American trade, and captured sailors were still liable to be treated as heretics by the Inquisition. His honourable scheme for a full union with Scotland was defeated by ignorance, prejudice and greed. The Commons were irritated by criticism made of them by Thornborough, Bishop of Bristol, and James's angry speech at the end of the first session shows how wide the misunderstandings already were. James never understood the arts of parliamentary management, and with many of the Privy Councillors now in the Lords, the debates were not properly controlled. Presently the Speaker, a royal nominee, would be told that he was a servant of the House, not 'a master's mate'. James allowed the Commons to develop a corporate identity by keeping his first Parliament for seven years, during which it met five times. Of Elizabeth's ten Parliaments only two met for more than one session.

The vital problem was finance. James was hopelessly extravagant, and his peacetime expenditure was soon as great as Elizabeth's in war. Subsidies had to be sought from Parliament no longer as grants for special purposes but as a necessary supplement to the ordinary revenue. The Commons were reluctant to make such grants to a conspicuous spendthrift whose policy was suspect in other ways, and requests for supply were habitually shelved for the more congenial business of discussing grievances. James sold lands worth more than £750,000 and the tithes in some 1,450 parishes, and improvements were made in the farming of the taxes, but the debt and the annual deficit steadily mounted. In 1606 the deficit was £81,000 and the Commons, in the brief harmony that followed the Gunpowder Plot, granted two subsidies. In the same year the merchant Bate refused to pay a duty on currants. His objection was to do with the privileges of the Levant Company and there was little sympathy for his particular case, but the legal issue was complex. The Crown had an admitted right to regulate trade in the national interest, and the duty on currants could be defended as an item in a commercial war with Venice. On the other hand, Customs formed part of the revenue, and the raising of revenue required the consent of Parliament. The judges ruled that by precedent the Crown had power to raise duties at the ports and had 'continually used this power notwithstanding all acts of Parliament against it'.

There was no immediate opposition to this decision and in 1608 Burghley's son, Robert Cecil, now Earl of Salisbury, tried to relieve the King's financial difficulties by issuing a revised Book of Rates to bring in an annual £70,000 a year. The duties were on luxuries and imported manufactures and Salisbury had obtained the approval of the City before imposing them. But these were manifestly impositions for the sake of revenue rather than economic regulation, and the Commons at once fell upon a source of income that might in time make the Crown financially independent. A mature and far-seeing speech by James Whitelocke in 1610 [14] claimed that all taxation was vested in the sovereign power, which was the King-in-Parliament, and not in either of them separately. This in effect was to assert the sovereignty of Parliament since without some independent sources of revenue the Crown could not govern.

The confusion over impositions helped to frustrate a larger plan for fiscal reform. In the 'Great Contract' Salisbury offered to surrender the Crown's ancient rights to wardship and purveyance for a lump sum. These were long-standing irritants. When military service had been a condition of land-holding, it had made sense for the Crown to receive during a minority a financial due with which to hire another knight. But by 1600 wardship was just an arbitrary form of death duty which fell on some families and not on others. Purveyance was the right to buy supplies for the royal household at less than the market price, and this was resented even though it ensured employment and turnover. Salisbury proposed to commute these and other minor dues for an annual £200,000, and he also asked for a grant of £600,000 to clear the Crown's debts. This arrangement would have brought the Crown an additional £100,000 a year and would have saved the taxpayer the fees and perquisites gathered by the collectors. At first there seemed to be some prospect of agreement, but on second thoughts James I was reluctant to surrender any part of his prerogative, and the Commons thought that they had offered too good a bargain and demanded that the King should withdraw impositions and make concessions in religion. The session ended stormily with a formidable petition on grievances, and a sensible financial accommodation was postponed for another fifty years. English landowners had given military service to the Crown, and in local government they were giving administrative service, sometimes at the cost of their own immediate interests, but their financial responsibility as taxpayers was something they would not yet accept.

James continued to levy impositions, although he was always promising to review them, but by 1613 there was a debt of half a million pounds and a deficit of £160,000. The funeral of the Prince of Wales was a costly ceremony and the wedding celebrations of Princess Elizabeth were even more lavish. In James's defence, such munificence was expected of a Renaissance prince, and many of Queen Elizabeth's subjects had found her frugality embarrassing. Courtiers and officials battened on the Crown, and James complained to his council that 'there are so many gapers, and so little to be spared'. His necessities compelled him to summon Parliament and perhaps, although the evidence is not very convincing, to try to procure the election of 'undertakers' pledged to support royal policy. The Addled Parliament, which was dismissed after nine weeks of wrangling, was probably wrecked quite deliberately by the Howards, who feared the Commons' Protestant hostility to Spain. Salisbury was dead and the session was 'managed' for the Crown by Winwood, an inexperienced bureaucrat who said afterwards that the first speech to which he ever listened in the Commons was his own.

Much had happened by the time Parliament met again in 1621. Gondomar, the Spanish ambassador, achieved great influence over the King by affecting to esteem his kingcraft as highly as he did himself. Raleigh, whose very name recalled more heroic times, was released from prison and given a gambler's chance to save himself by discovering gold in the Orinoco. His execution was Gondomar's pound of flesh. The Thirty Years War broke out when James's Protestant son-in-law, the Elector Palatine, accepted the crown of Bohemia and was rapidly expelled not only from his new kingdom but from his own electorate. Religious and patriotic feelings were outraged when in England the penal laws against the Catholics were relaxed and James I, after expressing dutiful concern for 'the state of religion through all Christendom, which almost wholly, under God, rests now upon my shoulders', proposed to marry Prince Charles to the Spanish Infanta. His idea was that for her dowry she should bring the Palatinate, which James would then restore to his grateful son-in-law.

This diplomatic imbecility inflamed Puritan feeling, which in recent years had been quietly consolidating under Abbot's tolerance and the somewhat devious leadership of John Preston. At Cambridge Preston had drawn large crowds to his Calvinist sermons and he had also been a very influential teacher. Already the friend of Puritan gentry like the Knightleys of Fawsley Hall and the Copes of Hanwell, he schemed to give Puritanism further respectability and influence by winning support among the aristocracy. Fulke Greville was his patron, and another useful ally was the Earl of Lincoln, one of his former pupils. He had a maxim that 'when we have any great things to be accomplished, the best policy is to work by an engine which the world sees nothing of'. The engine in question was Lord Saye and Sele, 'Old Subtlety', of whom Clarendon said that 'he had, with his milk, sucked in an implacable malice against the government of the Church . . . and was in truth the pilot that steered all those vessels which were freighted with sedition to destroy the government'. Preston found his way to court after impressing James in an academic disputation, and, through the influence of Buckingham, who was always agreeable to respectful suitors of any persuasion, he was appointed chaplain to Prince Charles. He helped to direct the

Puritan opposition in the Commons in 1621, and his influence was to become still greater when, after two disastrous sessions, Buckingham had his 'godly fit' and tried to win Puritan support.

James's poverty led to the Cockayne scandal in 1614. Sir William Cockayne, a London merchant, offered the Crown the huge sum of £300,000 a year for the exclusive right to export dressed cloth. In theory this was an acceptable scheme to recover the Baltic trade and reserve the profitable dressing process to English clothiers, and it was also welcomed as a blow at the privileges of the Merchant Adventurers. But Cockayne may have been only interested in a quick profit for himself, and his company lacked the necessary shipping and capital. The result was the over-production of cloth that could not be exported, with riots, bankruptcies and unemployment, although the government insisted on the weavers being paid their wages when there was no work for them to do. The trade took years to recover, and the affair was damaging alike to royal prestige and the policy of economic regulation.

In 1618, when the debt had risen to £900,000, James was temporarily reprieved by Lionel Cranfield, an efficient administrator who managed to balance the budget by economies in the household, the navy and the Court of Wards, but these reforms were achieved at the expense of greedy courtiers, and Buckingham soon found that they limited the patronage at his disposal. He welcomed economies in the navy when the senile Effingham was Lord High Admiral, but not when he succeeded to the office himself. There was further friction at court when in 1619 Cranfield was made Treasurer, a post that had been coveted by Coke. Another unpopular feature of the Crown's bid for solvency was a massive increase in monopolies and patents, which Elizabeth had promised to leave within the discretion of common law. By 1621 there were 700 of these, and their indiscriminate sale to courtiers and their dependants now had little to do with the provision of emoluments for deserving officials. A court monopoly of the manufacture of gold and silver thread was held to be responsible for a loss of bullion, and an exclusive permit for the licensing of ale-houses, while defensible as a police measure, encroached on the rights of local justices. Often, too, the monopolists' efforts to enforce their privileges led to riots and intimidation.

A further slump in the cloth trade in 1620 was felt over the whole of an increasingly capitalised and sensitive economy, and with the harvest failing as well, Parliament met to the mournful accompaniment of falling prices, reduced exports and starvation wages. Their overriding concern was for the safety of Protestantism with the Hapsburgs ready to start an offensive that would carry the Counter-Reformation to the North Sea and the Baltic. Papists were never more insolent, Sir Robert Phelips complained, adding with the confident insularity of English Puritanism, 'I beseech God, that chose this corner of the earth to plant His truth in, to preserve it'. It was known that the court itself was divided over foreign policy, as the Scottish group under Hamilton wanted an active alliance with France and Holland. The Commons were concerned, too, that apart from the brief and abortive session in 1614, this was the first Parliament for eleven years, and it was only the international emergency that had forced James to call it. It was always the Commons' greatest fear that the Crown would be able to get along without them, and the recent improvement in the royal finances was ominous. A renewed attack on monopolies and impositions was therefore inevitable. Since 1610 the Crown's credibility had been successively damaged by the Overbury murder, the respect shown for the ubiquitous Gondomar, the Cockayne fiasco, the sacrifice of Raleigh, the snubbing of the Sabbatarians in the Book of Sports (1618), apparent clemency to Catholic recusants, and the disrepute of a court dominated by Buckingham and his 'skip-jack' baronets. There was something very close to a loss of national confidence in the government, whose leader in the coming crisis was Buckingham, a man not yet brought into any contact with reality.

James I asked the Commons for half a million pounds for the emergency. They voted £160,000 and then turned to their grievances. The Sabbath was mentioned, and the recusancy laws, and during a complaint against the Merchant Adventurers it was stated on behalf of the Virginia Company that royal interference with trade was harmful to the new territories. The real assault was on the monopolists, and James I and Buckingham, anxious to placate the Commons and get their taxes, stood aside when the procedure of impeachment, not used since 1459, was revived against two of the more scandalous profiteers. They still offered no defence when Bacon, the Lord Chancellor, was impeached for the common practice of accepting gifts from litigants. They soon discovered that conciliation was no more effective than resistance, as the Commons went on to explain how the war should be conducted. Prince Charles should marry a Protestant princess and instead of military intervention on the Continent, they were in favour of an Elizabethan war of piracy to recover the Palatinate by privateering in the Caribbean, 'to enrich ourselves as well as to defend our right'. This was a direct challenge to the Crown, since royal marriages and foreign policy undoubtedly belonged to the prerogative. After an exchange of wordy petitions and wordy replies the Commons entered a protestation claiming a right to debate all 'arduous and urgent affairs' in the realm [15]. As they could refuse to finance policies they disliked, they were in effect demanding the direction of policy. James tore the protestation from their journal and sent them home.

The Puritans had taken care that London should have its fill of cautionary sermons during the session, and there were preachers 'continually progging at the Parliament door'. Buckingham had been impressed and frightened by the vigour of the Puritan opposition and he began seriously to consider putting himself at the head of it. Preston was offered a government post and a bishopric. These he refused, preferring the role of *éminence grise*, but in 1622 he was appointed Master of the Puritan nursery at Emmanuel and he also succeeded John Donne as preacher to the lawyers at Lincoln's Inn. The Puritan tactic was to persuade Buckingham, never strongly resistant to flattery, that his rapid rise to power was proof that he was the instrument of God's people. He should therefore oppose the Spanish marriage and allow himself to be guided by Parliament. A less spiritual inducement was the sale of the bishops' lands and the endowments of the cathedral choirs, from which it should be possible to pay the Crown's debts as well as reward the individually deserving.

These unsubtle negotiations were interrupted by Buckingham's journey to Spain to supervise Charles's wooing of the Infanta, on which James was still determined. This from the Puritan point of view was a test of Buckingham's real intentions, and it is possible that his celebrated boorishness in Spain was deliberately designed to wreck a policy which he knew could not succeed. He was already sounding the possibilities of a French marriage, and although he met an embarrassing obstacle in the Prince's brief infatuation with the Infanta, he finally achieved his object. He now demanded war, and in the Parliament of 1624 James virtually conceded everything for which he had previously fought. The Commons granted only half the money for which they were asked and appointed a committee to supervise the spending of it; Cranfield was impeached for opposing the war on account of the cost; naval operations were again urged in preference to Buckingham's plan for a campaign in Europe; and an Act against monopolies was the first statutory limitation of the prerogative since the fifteenth century. An English expedition was put under the command of Mansfeld, a wandering soldier of fortune, and the money allocated for it was spent before it left Dover. Three-quarters of the force died at Flushing of hunger and disease and it dispersed without striking a blow.

James had indeed discovered, as he had once warned his son, that 'the highest bench is sliddriest to sit upon'. Naïvely he told his last Parliament that 'never king was better beloved of his people than I am', but his ambitious kingcraft had entirely failed and it is difficult to see what remedies were now available to his successor. Whatever powers might belong to the prerogative, ultimate authority in England's 'mixed constitution' lay with the King-in-Parliament. If the two elements were in conflict, the Crown might find various expedients to postpone surrender, but that was all. It could not survive the financial and administrative stress of war.

The existence of certain portraits is apt to have an arbitrarily decisive effect on historical opinion, and posterity's view of Charles I has been influenced by Van Dyck's depiction of him; and of Strafford too, the dark, forbidding knight. Van Dyck, a masterly technician, was supremely the court painter who sensed how his sitters would like to appear and showed them thus. Apart from concealing Charles's humbling lack of inches, he painted him as a composed and dignified man of command. There is no suggestion of the hidden uncertainties. Charles died, when he could no longer avoid it, in defence of principles, honourable and sincerely held, which he had sometimes been willing to compromise. He had a stammer, and possibly he was late in maturing sexually; this made him diffident. He had an exalted view of his office, which taught him that he need not keep faith with subjects, and this led to prevarication, the tendency to 'squiborate'. His love of painting was the refuge of a man unequipped for the responsibilities which he none the less accepted with a dedicated courage. The public face appears in the acidulous, threatening address to Parliament in 1628 [16]; the real inadequate man in his Queen's exasperated letter when in 1642 he was roaming the country in search of friends, principles, policy, anything that would rescue him from his doubts [17].

The reign of Charles I began with the King's marriage to Henrietta Maria of France, with secret provisions for Catholics, and an outbreak of plague in which watchful Puritans saw evidence of divine displeasure. Buckingham, for whom success was always just round the corner, was looking for military glory and he had committed Charles to the support of Holland and Denmark in the war against the Emperor. But James I before his death had promised to lend Louis XIII replacements for six French ships that had been captured by Huguenot rebels, and Buckingham's intentions were suspect when these replacements were used in a successful attack on La Rochelle. The Parliament of 1625, meeting in Oxford, voted only £140,000 towards Charles's diplomatic commitments, and the Commons suggested that the best assurance of the nation's safety was to suppress the Catholics at home, which was not being done. They were critical of Richard Montagu, a wordy cleric whose *Appello Caesarem* (1625) combined Popish tendencies in religion with absolutism in politics, and in their fear of continued impositions they voted tonnage and poundage for one year only instead of for the whole reign as had been the recent practice. Charles had refused to disclose particulars of the foreign policy he was asking Parliament to support, but after the dissolution the whole country learned of the humiliation of a would-be Elizabethan raid on Cadiz. Some of the ships engaged in it had last seen active service against the Armada, and the soldiers' ammunition would not fit the rusted muskets.

Buckingham's hope of winning over the Commons by a spectacular victory had failed wretchedly, and it would seem that Preston and the Puritan group at court gave him his last chance at a conference held in February 1626. To test the sincerity of his policies they wanted him in particular to renounce Montagu and to recognise the Calvinist resolutions of the Synod of Dort (1618–19) as the essential doctrine of the Church of England. *Post hoc propter hoc* is unsound historical reasoning, especially in a situation as confused as this, but the frontal attack on Buckingham began only after the failure of this conference. He had been criticised before, but now he was 'the moth of all goodness' and to save him from impeachment, Charles had to dissolve the 1626 Parliament with the ominous reminder that 'Parliaments are altogether in my power for their calling, sitting and dissolution; therefore, as I find the fruits of them good or evil, they are to continue or not to be'.

If he had not been assassinated Buckingham might have courted the Puritans again in 1628, when he was proving his staunch Protestantism by helping the Huguenots, but he was forced away from them now by his master's affection for prelacy. After some years with no very positive religious convictions, Charles had been aesthetically and imaginatively attracted to the system loosely known as Arminian. Arminius himself, who died in 1609, believed in free will as against the irresistibility of grace and the final perseverance of the elect. In Holland the religious dispute was linked with politics and the question whether the Dutch should declare war on Spain. Oldenbarneveldt and Grotius were among the supporters of Arminius when his views were formally condemned at Dort. In England, too, the significance of the movement was partly political, but the English Arminians—as the Puritans specifically called them, and the term has to be accepted—tended to be 'broad church' in a refusal to dogmatise about predestination, and in this respect they were less positive than Baro and Barret at Cambridge in the 1590s. Lancelot Andrewes, possibly the earliest of them, urged an 'apostolic handsomeness and order', and they did not think that churches should be stripped bare to become mere auditoria for the preaching of the Word. They believed that the sacraments and a disciplined ceremonial had their place in Christian worship, they accepted the divine institution of episcopacy, and when they intervened in politics they mostly held 'Establishment' views. To the Puritans this was just the Scarlet Whore wearing a new transparent guise, and with Laud, 'that little active wheel', busily moving Arminians into all the best preferments, relations between Crown and Parliament came inevitably to breaking-point. It is impossible to distinguish between religious and constitutional motives. Sir John Eliot can best testify to that: 'It is observable in the House of Commons ... that wherever that mention does break forth of the fears or dangers in religion, and the increase of Popery, their affections are much stirred; and whatever is obnoxious in the State, it then is reckoned as an incident to that'.

After the dissolution in 1626 and the rout of his Danish allies at Lutter, Charles I went on with his military schemes and Buckingham managed to be drawn into a war with France, theoretically his most hopeful ally against Spain. He himself led an expedition against the island of Rhé, not without personal gallantry, but forty English flags later hung in Notre Dame (1627). A fleet under Denbigh in the following year sailed home again without even testing the strength of Richelieu's fortifications. Levies were extracted from the counties to train the militia, and ships or ship-money were demanded from the ports; tonnage and poundage were collected by prerogative; troops were billeted in private houses; and the rights of local justices were infringed by commissions of martial law which involved jurisdiction over soldiers and civilians alike. Finally, Charles demanded a forced loan equivalent to five subsidies, and the Laudian clergy were commanded to preach non-resistance. Sibthorpe, preaching before the judges, stretched the doctrine of apostolic obedience to include the payment of forced loans, and Manwaring said that 'all the significations of a royal pleasure are ... in the nature and force of a command', even when 'flatly against the law of God'. Several of the gentry were imprisoned for refusing to pay the loans, and in Darnel's case the judges decided that men so imprisoned were not bailable: 'if no cause of the commitment be expressed, it is to be presumed to be for matters of state, which we cannot take notice of'. The judges would adopt the same line when merchants were imprisoned for refusing to pay tonnage and poundage.

With all these accumulating abuses the Commons opened their meeting in 1628 with a fast for the country's sins, which set up 'a wall of separation between God and us'. Five subsidies were voted but held in committee while the Commons tried to restrain the King's actions within the bounds of acknowledged law. The Petition of Right was an assertion of ancient principles and really settled nothing. The same is true of Pym's speech during the impeachment of Manwaring [18], a classic exposition of the balanced constitution from which the equipoise had in fact departed, and disingenuous in its failure to admit that his parliamentary colleagues had done far more to destroy the balance than an over-exuberant cleric like Manwaring. Attempts to include in the Petition a saving clause to safeguard the Crown's prerogatives in emergency were defeated by Coke's legalistic conservatism and the Commons' basic mistrust of Charles. By the autumn session Buckingham, 'the grievance of grievances', had been removed by assassination, and if politics had been the only issue it might have been possible to reach a working agreement. But Laud was now Bishop of London, Abbot no longer counted, the Queen was flaunting her Popery, and Arminians, including Montagu, were entrenched in the best bishoprics and deaneries; while on the Continent La Rochelle was falling and Tilly and Wallenstein had Protestantism by the throat. In the Commons the noisiest cry was about merchants burdened with illegal impositions, but religion was the cause that unified the opposition. These financial devices might enable the Crown to dispense with Parliament and silently lead the country back in the direction of Rome. Parliament in this sense had become the instrument of God's people, and the Puritans themselves the voice of an oppressed nation.

When Charles ordered an adjournment, Eliot and others staged what was probably a pre-arranged demonstration. Holding the Speaker in his chair, they passed, by acclamation, resolutions condemning religious innovations, the extension of Popery and Arminianism, and the payment of tonnage and poundage. Eliot and eight others went to prison, and Parliament did not meet again for eleven years.

2

War and Beyond

Though in the trade of war I have slain men,
Yet do I hold it very stuff o' the conscience
To do no contriv'd murder.

OTHELLO I ii 1

Sir John Eliot's performance in 1629 was so irresponsible that Charles I
had a case when he complained, on dissolving Parliament, of 'some few
vipers' who had cast a 'mist of undutifulness' over the House of Commons. He had tried to work with Parliament, and he would be 'more
inclinable' to do so again when 'our people shall see more clearly into
our intentions and actions'. There is no evidence that he was consciously
proposing a sort of rule that in contemporary terms could be called a
despotism. He saw it rather as his duty to protect the country from the
unconstitutional pretensions of extremists who would 'erect an universal
over-swaying power to themselves', and until the issue of ultimate
sovereignty was resolved this was not an improper attitude. As long as
he could stay out of war and develop the financial resources that still lay
within the prerogative, Charles could keep going. Until his opponents
drove him into extreme positions, it is unlikely that he intended anything
else. It had, after all, been Elizabeth's policy whenever she could afford
it.

The Scottish rebellion only hastened the collapse of an improvised system that must eventually have broken down through the withdrawal of
co-operation by taxpayers and local administrators. Its survival depended chiefly upon inertia, and here the doves were wiser than the hawks.
Both Laud and Strafford were so positive and articulate that the actual
effectiveness of the policy of 'Thorough' has probably been overesti-
mated. They knew what they wanted but it is doubtful how far they
achieved it, and their correspondence shows their own misgivings about
this. Similarly, it was the fear of what they might do, rather than anything they had actually done, that caused the Commons' virulent attack
upon them in 1641. Laud's bustle at the centre had relatively little effect

on the periphery of ecclesiastical affairs, where secular influence in the parish system had always tended to be impervious to the efforts of authority. Strafford was never admitted to the centre as Charles could not bring himself to forgive or trust a man who had once hounded Buckingham and gone to prison for resisting a forced loan. In the Council of the North, and later in Ireland, Strafford made powerful enemies by relieving the poor from the oppressions of the gentry, establishing comparatively honest government and enforcing the traditional economic paternalism of the Crown. His political beliefs were conservative: *stare super vias antiquas*, 'tread the old and wonted boards', through a constructive co-operation between Crown and Parliament. In the crisis of 1640 he gave the orthodox advice that Parliament should be summoned. But, like Bacon before him, he thought that if co-operation should break down it would be necessary to trust the executive: 'the authority of a king is the keystone which closeth up the arch and order of government'. For this reason he had changed sides in 1628, convinced that certain elements in the Commons were determined on disruption when the Petition of Right had given an opportunity for harmony and understanding. In Ireland a natural imperiousness of temper was aggravated by ill-health, and he grew increasingly high-handed in his financial extortions, the pressure on juries, the impatience with obstructive lawyers and officials, and the arrogant clash with the City over their Londonderry charter. Strafford therefore won a reputation as a man ruthless in the royal interest, and additionally the parliamentarians always hated him as a renegade. But his 'Thorough', exercised in distant places, made little impact on the court, where there was always someone ready to listen to the complaints of his influential victims. Charles was incapable of a settled policy about anything, while courtiers such as Weston, Cottington and Windebank, all Catholics or nearly so, were more anxious to avoid conflict than to stand forth as champions of strong government.

In finance Charles was always in sight of solvency without ever achieving it. He made immediate peace with France and Spain, but there were still war debts to be paid. The court was not extravagant. Weston and Juxon, the successive Treasurers, made administrative economies, the sale of lands and offices continued as before, and the merchants abandoned their struggle against impositions. By various expedients the Crown's income rose above £800,000, but the debt and expenditure went up too and Charles was constantly raising loans in the City by mortgaging future revenue. It was the spendthrift's well-trodden road to disaster, because as soon as he had milked one source of income he had to find another, until eventually he arrived at ship-money. It was a minor irritant when every freeholder with land above £40 a year was compelled by an ancient statute to accept the dues of knighthood or compound for his refusal. Commissions were set up to reclaim land occupied by defective titles or by the enclosure of wastes or by encroachment on royal forests. The limits of the royal forests had been fixed by a perambulation in 1297, and by invoking this Charles was able to exact compensation from occupiers whose families had held and developed the land for generations. Monopolies, revived under a clause in the Act of 1624 which permitted the issue of patents to corporations, had the usual effect of raising prices and hampering commercial initiative. Heavy fines in the prerogative courts were thought to be primarily financial in motive, and even the privileged trading companies were alienated when Charles casually granted charters to their rivals. Charles's financial measures were unpopular not only because they were unparliamentary and of questionable legality. Most of them were also restrictive of trade and of economic expansion.

Ship-money was an ancient levy on the maritime counties for the defence of the realm and the suppression of piracy, and its collection in 1634 roused little opposition. In the next year it was extended to the whole country, which again was not unprecedented in an emergency, but the taxpayer began to ask what was the emergency, who was to be the judge of it, and what was being done with the money. Certainly there was a case for strengthening England's naval defences, as the combatants in the Thirty Years War were fighting their battles in English waters, English fishing-grounds were at the mercy of the Dutch, and merchant shipping was being attacked by privateers from Dunkirk and the Barbary coast. Even the coal ships from Newcastle were sometimes unable to reach London. Recognition of this weakness would explain the general readiness to pay ship-money in the early years, but it soon began to have the ominous appearance of a regular annual tax on land, which the Commons had always striven to prevent. There was some suspicion, too, that English ships were being used in Spanish interests, and, in so far as Charles had a foreign policy at all in the 1630s, it was thought to be Catholic in sympathy. Prynne said quite simply that ship-money was a tax to finance the setting up of idolatry. Meeting at Saye's house at Broughton, the opposition caucus decided to fight a test case (1637–8) in which John Hampden's counsel argued that even if there were an emergency, Parliament was 'the ordinary means of supply upon extraordinary occasions' and on this occasion there had been plenty of time to summon Parliament as the proper authority to decide whether an emergency existed. The judges on the whole took the line already adopted in the cases of Bate and Darnel, that these were matters of state in which they could not interfere, and no statute could limit the King's right and duty to defend the nation as he thought fit. Clarendon pointed out that a logical extension of this principle 'left no man anything he might call his own', and that the judges discredited themselves 'by being made use of in this and like acts of power'. The law—the common law this time, not just the prerogative courts and the bishops' courts—was falling into disrepute. Two judges, Heath and Richardson, had recently been disgraced for disputing royal policies. Eliot had died in the Tower, and Strode and Valentine, two of his accomplices in 1629, were still in prison, along with sundry pamphleteers who had been criticising Laud. It appeared that neither parliamentary privilege nor the processes of common law could protect a man from the King's displeasure. The judgment on Hampden brought the first serious signs of a taxpayer's revolt. In 1638 the yield from ship-money fell to less than two-thirds of the comparatively small sum demanded. In the following year the levy was much higher at £214,000, of which only £43,000 was paid, it being probable that the money would be spent not on naval defence but on military operations against the Scots, whom Laud had driven into revolt.

Laud was not the Papist that his enemies said he was, but he held the Arminian position that Rome, although grievously in error, was a part of the Catholic Church to which Anglicans also belonged, and that many of the so-called Reformed Churches were heretical and schismatic. Puritans lived a devout life because they were assured of grace, not in order that they might achieve it, and they were outraged by Laud's insistence upon ceremonial and liturgical rites that seemed to revive the idolatry and sacerdotalism of the Middle Ages. Arminians, on the other hand, could discover neither joy nor merit in worshipping the Creator in a converted cowshed. ' 'Tis superstition nowadays for any man to come with more reverence into a church than a tinker and his bitch into an alehouse.' 'The beauty of holiness', Laud's finest expression of his faith, had to be protected from that open scorn for the House of God by which many conscientious men proclaimed the inward worship that was in their hearts. Laud agreed that inward worship was 'the true service of God', and no service was acceptable without it, but he cherished ceremonies as 'the hedges that fence the substance of religion from all the indignities which profaneness and sacrilege too commonly put upon it'. In many parishes the Communion table was kept in the body of the church and used by the congregation as a hat-rack. Laud insisted upon a railed altar at the east end, and he also ordered the clergy to use the vestments apparently prescribed in the Injunctions of 1559. Ornaments reappeared in the churches, the money-lenders were ejected from a St Paul's partly rebuilt by Inigo Jones, and the worship of God was once again enriched by what Bishop Jewel had called its scenic apparatus.

Many English Arminians, possibly even Laud himself, were still moderately Calvinist in theology, and no one at this time was persecuted for his beliefs. Most of the hierarchy supported Laud in his efforts to secure outward conformity. He had energetic adjutants in Neile at York, Curle at Winchester, Juxon at London, Wren, Montagu, Manwaring, Field (son of the famous Puritan preacher and brother of an actor in Shakespeare's company) and Cosin, a Prebendary of Durham and Master of Peterhouse. There was also Richard Corbet [19], the second-best poet (although by some distance) among the Caroline bishops, who 'sang ballads at the cross at Abingdon on a market-day' and harried the Puritans of East Anglia because he found them such mournful asses. Laud prohibited discussion of 'deep points' of the Christian faith, censored Puritan writings, forbade the gentry to keep private chaplains or corporations to appoint lecturers for preaching duties only. He hunted disobedient clergy from their pulpits and extended his interference to the refugee churches at home, and to English settlers, merchant communities and regiments overseas. Laud had no personal graces to soften the effect of his intrusions, but for all the pettiness and unwisdom, the chivvying of psychopaths who were better left alone, his aims were not contemptible. This was the last effort of Anglicanism to hold all men's loyalty to a single unified Church that should be coextensive with society.

It is difficult, however, to know what success it actually achieved, especially as the noisiest evidence comes from the men who defeated it. There was much exaggeration in the charges brought against some of the fallen bishops after 1640. Some of it was inspired by personal vindictiveness, like Prynne's vendetta against Laud or the attack on Cosin by Peter Smart, a Puritan whom he had ejected from a Durham prebend. Wren, accused by the Commons of 'setting up idolatry and superstition in divers places, and acting some things of that nature in his own person', was kept in the Tower for eighteen years. The Arminian belief in reason and tradition offended Puritan individualism, with its preference for blinding illuminations, and it was easy to brand all Arminians as Papists. Selden admitted that this was a bogus smear 'to make them odious', but the moderate Falkland thought that, although not a Roman Popery, Arminianism was a new sort of English Popery designed to make the people dependent on the clergy. The Puritans used the word 'innovations' to describe measures which had not been used in England since the Reformation, and these, according to d'Ewes, 'ensaddled the souls of all who had any true piety'. For the first time men began to glory in the name of Puritan. The sects silently multiplied with the attachment of believers who had lost all confidence in a national Church, while more active spirits went off to join the Protestant armies in Europe or to found their own communities in Holland or America.

But life away from the centre probably continued much as before, as indeed it had done throughout a hundred years of religious unsettlement. Arminianism could inspire much piety and learning, but mostly this was from educated men. It could never, by its nature, be a 'popular' faith. It tended to be remote and intellectual, and its call to the devout life had little of the Puritan fire. Laud had found inadequate support among the uncomprehending parish clergy, who mostly followed their patrons' bidding; or if they did not, a lecturer or circuit preacher would undo their work in the afternoon and, Laud feared, 'blow the bellows of sedition'. Stratford, which had had a Puritan corporation since the 1560s, is always interesting evidence. There the vicar from 1619 to 1638 was Thomas Wilson, an eloquent preacher but in other respects an imbecile who even strained the loyalty of his Puritan congregation. He kept pigs and poultry in the newly-restored chancel, and dried his children's washing there. From 1629 his churchwarden was Dr John Hall, who was married to Shakespeare's daughter Susanna. As a physician Hall knew something of the vitamin cure for scurvy, the bane of contemporary sailors, and he was well esteemed by the local gentry. They knew him as a thorough-going Puritan, and his wife's epitaph said that if Mistress Hall was 'wise to salvation', she owed this more to her husband than to her father. Parish records show Hall as churchwarden behaving almost as a Genevan lay elder, reproving the citizenry for 'loitering forth of church on sermontime', 'sleeping in the belfry, with his hat on, upon the Sabbath', sitting unreverently in church and 'laughing and rumbling' during the service. Laud or no, Stratford in the 1630s was still going its own way, just as it had when in 1622 the King's Men, coming to see Janssen's bust of their late colleague newly erected in the church, were forbidden by the corporation to act a play. Local records will also show a remarkable variety of practice even within a small area. At Uppingham, in Rutland, the rector was Jeremy Taylor, later to be a chaplain to the royal army, a celebrated Anglican preacher and author of *Holy Living* and *Holy Dying*, but just down the hill at Lyddington, Richard Rudd, vicar from 1591 to 1649, completed in 1635 massive four-sided rails which would have kept the Communion table firmly anchored in the body of the church.

Thus the extent of Laudianism should probably not be judged only by the outcry of its noisier victims. The threat was usually worse than the deed, and Puritanism was too firmly entrenched to be disturbed. Even the unpopular Book of Sports, re-issued in 1633, was disregarded in areas where Sabbatarianism had taken root. Except from the King, Laud had no encouragement from the court, where the Catholic Henrietta Maria and her Massing priests were his bitter enemies. Like all Stuart policies, his ambitions foundered ultimately on lack of money and the opposition of the gentry. Although he was sincerely anxious to reform the Church, his own instruments were corrupt since simony and pluralism had to continue if the clergy were to be adequately paid. (This objective has yet to be achieved. In 1973 57 per cent of incumbents were receiving stipends below the modest figure of £1,650 which a recent commission had declared to be an essential minimum.) Laud suppressed the feoffees for impropriations, a trust established by the Puritans in 1626 to consolidate the various legacies and bequests given for the maintenance of the clergy. Some of the money was used to augment the stipends and maintain lecturers and students, but the principal objects were to buy back lay impropriations and to provide an adequate wage. Laud had them suppressed in 1633 as an illegal corporation and confiscated their assets, because he rightly saw that their object was political: they were planting their ministers in parliamentary boroughs with a view to influencing the elections. But the feoffees were in theory trying to do what everyone agreed needed to be done, and Laud himself achieved a modest success here. He aimed to buy two impropriations a year through fines collected in High Commission, and he made the bishops exercise their legal right to compel impropriators to supplement inadequate livings. Vicars were encouraged to petition the Privy Council, and a number of lay patrons and corporations were forced to pay better stipends. This was not unreasonable as many vicars were still receiving only about 15 per cent of the value of the impropriation, but it brought Laud into conflict with the sacred rights of property. He hoped eventually to impose this obligation on all who had inherited monastery lands, and if he could obtain the support of the common law, fines for leases, impropriations and dubious titles might become a regular source of income like shipmoney. Montagu, who incidentally was seeking to revive the Catholic doctrine of purgatory, contemplated the eventual resumption by the Church of all the monastic revenues; and it was noted that in Ireland Bishop Bramhall had recovered leases and impropriations to the value of £30,000 a year.

The threat to property, and to the local jurisdictions it conferred, jeopardised the whole of Laud's policy, and when he turned his attentions to Scotland, his ruin was swift. Believing as he did in one uniform Church for the whole kingdom, it was inevitable that he should determine to bring the Scots within the national system. James I and Bancroft had already enlarged the rights and duties of the bishops, and in 1625 Charles I imposed an Act of Revocation which recovered all ecclesiastical lands and tithes acquired by laymen since 1542. This enabled ministers to receive a competent wage, but in sensitive Protestant eyes it was soon to have a disturbing counterpart in the Edict of Restitution which the Emperor imposed on northern Europe in 1629. Having visited Scotland and observed the disordered variety of its public worship, Laud saw the need for a uniform liturgy, and he decided to impose the English service-book in preference to one submitted by the Scottish bishops. Superseding Knox's Book of Common Order, it was introduced by proclamation in 1637 without prior consultation of the native Parliament or the General Assembly. Strafford was causing anxiety by his treatment of the Scots settlers in Ulster, and this further affront to religion, patriotism and the constitution had the effect of allying the anti-clerical nobility with the Presbyterian Kirk. No minister dared use the hated book or the vestments prescribed with it, and in 1638 the Scots signed a National Covenant pledging themselves to resist until it had been withdrawn. Later in the year a Church Assembly, ominously elected on a Genevan model, declared the abolition of episcopacy.

Charles went the whole gamut between coercion and concession, as he would do for the rest of his life. Indecision was his fatal fault, rather than duplicity, but the two were often indistinguishable and there is a point where indecision becomes a moral disease. His enemies always supposed that when he made a concession, he intended to revoke it when he could, and this personal mistrust of the King is a constant factor in the crises of the next ten years. Immediately, however, there was a collapse of confidence in the whole regime. As soon as pressure was applied, the government discovered how few friends they had anywhere, and they had to face the accumulated grievances of a decade of personal rule. Illegal taxation, now taking a permanent form, was perhaps the loudest, but not everyone paid taxes and the Puritans exploited the common fear that Protestantism was now in danger here in England, not only on the Continent. They were able to show, too, that the pseudo-Papist Arminians were preaching absolutism from their pulpits, and although in Europe the danger to religion was now receding, no true Protestant liked being rescued by Richelieu, an ally of the hated Catholic Queen. The complaints of the lawyers were more technical, but lawyers were articulate men who could see where the present policies of the courts and judges might lead. Most significant of all was the desertion of the City. Charles could not raise sufficient loans for his campaigns against the Scots, and between 1639 and 1641 he lost the support of the London merchants who, as the Crown's principal creditors, were most closely concerned in the continuance of its policies. Even the monopolist companies, enriched by royal charters, began to change their allegiance. In his need for money Charles had multiplied his grants of economic privileges, and so made them less exclusive. Interlopers had been admitted, and charters had been erratically withdrawn or reconstituted, with the result that the merchants seem to have decided that their trade would never prosper with these continued and unpredictable vexations. They saw the need for a new fiscal system, and thus for a political settlement that would make it possible.

Pym and other leaders of the Commons had kept in touch during the 1630s as directors of a company for 'the plantation of Providence, Henrietta and the Adjacent Islands'. (One of the settlements was to be called Sayebrook, but it was never planted.) Presbyterianism was not in itself a popular cause in England, and the dramatists still saw the comic side of it [20], but the Scots rebellion was too good an opportunity to miss. After a truce with the King at Berwick in 1639, the Scots were privately encouraged to maintain a military presence, and on Strafford's advice Charles summoned Parliament in the following spring with a request for money for the defence of the kingdom. Appealing to the Commons' entrenched respect for legal and antiquarian precedent, Pym replied with a recital of the liberties violated by recent abuses of the prerogative. Redress of grievances was, in the traditional manner, to precede supply. Charles dissolved the Parliament after only three weeks, in itself a tactical error because he had not given time for the Commons' early euphoric unity to develop its inevitable fractures. For Pym, the session was a triumph for a man who never discovered the difference between tactics and strategy. Six months later Charles was delivered into his hands following a renewed attack upon the Scots which was ignominiously brushed aside at Newburn-on-Tyne. The clergy had only made things worse by voting a financial contribution and enacting canons against disobedience to royal commands. After a futile recourse to the mediaeval device of a Council of Peers, Charles was obliged in November 1640 to summon the Long Parliament to get financial endorsement of his undertaking to pay the Scots army £850 a day as a condition of their not living on the countryside or molesting the coal-trade from Newcastle.

At the elections Pym organised the strenuous propaganda of Puritan preachers, Hampden was carried round the country as a sort of totem, and the return of only one government supporter from the royal duchy of Cornwall indicated the temper of the nation. Shielded by the Scots army in the north—there could be no fear of dissolving Parliament, said Baillie, a Covenanting chaplain, 'so long as the lads about Newcastle sit still'—the Commons passed during the first half of 1641 a series of measures to strip the Crown of its exceptional powers and ended for ever its opportunities for personal rule. Ship-money, impositions and the prerogative courts, including High Commission, the special agency of royal supremacy in the Church, were swept away. A Triennial Act stated that no more than three years should pass without the summoning of Parliament, and an emergency measure, passed to safeguard the loans raised by the Commons to pay the Scottish army a 'brotherly assistance' of £300,000 a year, provided that the present Parliament should not be dissolved without its own consent. Almost unawares these two measures incorporated Parliament as a permanent and indispensable element of the constitution, which, against an unfettered royal prerogative of summoning and dissolving, it had never been before. They also assumed, more doubtfully, the willingness of the members to bear the inconvenience and expense—and London rents were always raised during sessions—of lengthy attendance to carry out their business. This work of decentralisation and destruction had made effective government impossible until the lost prerogatives should be accepted by someone else. Pym was inhibited by his past professions of constitutional propriety from specifically claiming them for Parliament. The issue of ultimate sovereignty was still in theory unresolved until events forced Parliament to presume it.

With deliberate encouragement from the Commons leaders, the meeting of the Long Parliament had been greeted with cathartic demonstrations of extremist opinion. Puritan preachers hailed Parliament as the instrument chosen for the erection of God's kingdom. Thomas Case bade them 'reform the universities . . . reform the cities . . . the countries . . . the Sabbath . . . the ordinances, the worship of God. Every plant which my heavenly Father hath not planted shall be rooted up'. Tradesmen addicted to religion pointed for their neighbours the exalted paths they should follow, women preachers invaded the pulpits, disbanded soldiers looted the churches, and Adamites proclaimed man's primitive innocence by going naked in the streets. In a surfeit of religious exhortation the Commons were summoned to repeated visions of Sion's coming glory, and there were exuberant expressions of that strain in Puritanism that had been kept dormant during the years of official repression, the belief that the day was at hand when Christ would reign for a thousand years and, after the journeymen had done their necessary work, the elect few, the saints, would share His splendour [21]. With this went plainer intimations of what the programme would involve: appropriation of 'the very greenness of the land', not just the cathedrals and the estates of the bishops but tithes, advowsons, the parson's freehold, lay patronage—the whole traditional structure of society.

Alarm at these extravagances began to create the divisions which, within a year of the Commons' united action against the Crown's prerogatives, would provide Charles with a party and means to fight a war. The gap was widened by the proceedings against Strafford, whom Pym knew he must remove as the only man strong enough to nerve Charles into positive action. Impeachment had to be dropped, despite Pym's unwarrantable argument that Strafford's several misdemeanours amounted to cumulative treason and St John's plea that beasts of prey and vermin do not deserve the protection of the law. Attainder was a simpler procedure, and Essex laconically remarked that 'Stone dead hath no fellow'. When the bill went to the Lords, Pym called out his pickets and carried it through a decimated House by sheer intimidation. Finally he extracted Charles's signature through fears for the safety of the Queen and her children. Everyone knew that it was judicial murder, and it caused a reaction even among many who were glad enough to see Strafford out of the way. Among other effects it was a blow to the prestige of the Lords, who might have recovered some of their vanishing authority by acting as the nation's arbiter between Crown and Commons; and it drove Charles into an apathy of self-reproach in which he accepted the subsequent measures restricting his prerogative. In the same month as Strafford (May 1641) died the Earl of Bedford, a Puritan and an opponent of the Crown who had latterly been admitted to the Privy Council in the hope that he would exercise a healing influence. Clarendon says that he died 'much afflicted with the passion and fury which he perceived his party inclined to', and he 'feared the rage and madness of this Parliament would bring more prejudice and mischief to the kingdom than it had ever sustained by the long intermission of parliaments'. His authority among the Puritan peers unfortunately passed to Saye, who fed on intrigue as his daily bread.

Bedford might have achieved the sort of settlement that the moderates desired, a working relationship with the Crown based on the recent constitutional reforms. It was possible to argue that these reforms had merely removed certain undesirable practices that had grown up under the Tudors and had recently been abused by the King's advisers, but religion was a more contentious issue, and in the absence of an agreed programme of reform the Commons leaders allowed it to drift dangerously. They were embarrassed by the importunity of their own supporters, with the Scots commissioners in London urging a Presbyterian system, and the City congregations, so useful to Parliament in other respects, expecting more radical changes. Now that the Laudians had been driven out, some kind of modified episcopacy would probably have satisfied most of the country, but it would be difficult to get agreement on the details: 'I can tell you, sir, what I would not have,' Cromwell remarked on this matter, 'but not what I would.' Meanwhile the removal of the bishops' discipline had led in many places to iconoclasm and the breakdown of established worship, and if they would not trust the King, Parliament should have given a positive lead. But it was Pym's policy to play down religion as an issue likely to arouse disagreement among the Commons when there were greater prizes to be won. He had always been primarily concerned with political objectives, using religion only when it was a safe and convenient way of gaining support. So although reforms were debated in both Houses, nothing came of them. The Commons quietly dropped a bill, based on the 'root and branch' petition of 15,000 Londoners, for the extirpation of episcopacy and amendments in the Prayer Book; and a less drastic scheme failed in the Lords, who also refused to abolish the temporal jurisdiction of bishops and exclude them from the House. In face of the radical visionaries, men of property appreciated the social advantages of the traditional government of the Church.

In August, 1641, when reform was losing its momentum, Charles went to Edinburgh to try to win the Scottish army to his side in return for concessions in religion. It was an unlikely enterprise, and it threw doubt on his willingness to co-operate in a constitutional settlement, especially when he tried to arrest Argyll and other opposition nobles. It was a disastrous step in another way, because in his four-month absence the Commons set up a Council of Defence, collected taxes, and ruled by ordinance. They showed that government could be carried on without the King.

This became particularly significant when, in October, a Catholic rebellion broke out in Ulster, the consequence of years of oppression but provoked immediately by the men who had been dismantling Strafford's policies. Stone dead had found a fellow after all. The rebellion raised the issue of military command, and indeed of ultimate executive control. Charles, suspected of intrigues in Scotland and complicity in the Irish rebellion, could not be allowed to appoint the commanders of an army which he might turn against the liberties of Parliament. Pym accordingly drew up the Grand Remonstrance, an appeal to the nation against the King which the Commons had been contemplating for some time. Mostly it was a deplorable document, trivial, inaccurate and emotionally over-charged. In its few constructive proposals it vaguely demanded the appointment of ministers 'such as the Parliament may have cause to confide in', and a synod of English and foreign (i.e. Scottish) divines was to confer on the 'intended reformation' of the Church. But in case any-one should take alarm, it was not intended to 'let loose the golden reins of discipline and government in the Church, to leave private persons or particular congregations to take up what form of Divine Service they please'. Pym was still trying to keep religion in the background and restore the unity of Parliament, but the time for opportunism was past. With swords drawn, the Remonstrance was carried in the Commons by only 159 votes to 148, and Charles, who had recently announced that he would live and die 'for the doctrine and discipline of the Church of England', had found a cause to fight for.

Edward Hyde, Falkland and other moderates urged him now to take his stand on the defence of the law, the Church and the constitution, but after a triumphant return to London his expectations were disappointed by the success of the radicals in the elections to the common council of the City. The oligarchic rule of merchant aldermen was undermined by the propaganda of Puritan clergy such as Calamy and Cornelius Burges, and the revolt of dissident members of the chartered companies. A Com-mittee of Public Safety was to be set up in London to establish a citizen militia for the City's defence against Popery and absolutism. Howling mobs were in the streets again, and in January 1642, Charles committed the folly of marching with an armed guard to the Commons to try to arrest Pym and four other members. The failure was even more humili-ating than the attempt, and within a week Charles had left London. From Windsor, and presently from York, he allowed Hyde to appeal to the sense and justice of the nation, while in London the Commons were forced into the irregular assumption of executive power. Still shrinking from an outright assertion of sovereignty, they made a specious attempt to distinguish between the office of monarchy and the immediate incum-bent. In the paper war in the first half of 1642, both sides seem to have been more intent on justifying their position than on looking for a settle-ment. If the Nineteen Propositions in June, which would have taken from the Crown more than was conceded in 1689, was designed to win converts for Parliament, it probably had the reverse effect. Charles in-creasingly won support in the natural reaction from an unsettled and revolutionary period. In March, the Militia Ordinance put the armed forces under parliamentary control, and in the first positive act of war Parliament strengthened the garrison of Hull, which would have been valuable to Charles as a port for foreign reinforcements and as an arsenal stocked with munitions intended for the Scottish wars. Charles, characteristically, arrived too late and was refused admission. When at midsummer both sides issued commissions of array, it was for thousands of Englishmen a cruel moment of decision.

Like a later war, this one was certain to be 'over by Christmas', because initially both sides believed that a single battle would bring their opponents to their senses and open realistic negotiations. If the battle of Edgehill had been at all decisive either way, this might well have happened. There is the curious fact that the Royalists were on average ten years younger than the rebels, suggesting perhaps that the rebels had spent their formative years under the influence of Elizabethan Puritanism. This seems to be the only undeniable, clear-cut distinction, but there are many possible ones: court versus country; the unending contest between ins and outs; gentry going up and gentry coming down; a demoralised aristocracy padding like dinosaurs in search of their old hunting-grounds; the cultural cleavage between pious household and corrupt hierarchy; the warfare of class against the bastions of privilege; expansionist merchants impatient of a restrictive economy; Puritan individualism fighting the ancient shibboleths of 'neighbourhood' and subordination; the Puritan religious ideal in conflict with a Church so imperfectly reformed that it was indistinguishable from Rome. All these are valid explanations, but none is complete. The conflict was partly social, but many of the privileged classes fought against their own economic interests where some stronger interest prevailed. It was partly religious, and convinced Puritans fought for Parliament; but as had happened for a time under Elizabeth, some lay Puritan opinion was disturbed by the extremists and became cautiously conservative. Waller's religious convictions were strong enough to decide his allegiance, but hundreds felt as he did that this was a 'war without an enemy' [22] and avoided a decision for as long as they were able. This sense of the war as a tragic and avoidable disaster goes far to explain the blurred divisions. The Hampshire vicar who prayed 'O Lord, in Thee have I trusted, Let me never be a Roundhead' was another who knew where he stood, but for many there was no single cause powerful enough to compel unquestioning adherence. This again is why local influences were so important. Old territorial rivalries were renewed, new upstart families contested counties with those in ancient possession, and magnates who armed their tenants as for a mediaeval affray brought them back to the fields when there was a harvest to be gathered in.

Finally, allegiances were confused because the war was about means, not ends. The common agreement between the two parties was much more important than their differences. No one wanted to revive Laudianism or ship-money or the recent abuses of the prerogative courts, and it was agreed that Parliament was an essential part of the constitution. Apart from sectaries who had abandoned the national Church, and perhaps a few visionaries who saw in the war a means to radical reconstruction, all the combatants clung to the old ideal of religious and political unity buttressed by an unchanging social order. Hooker had said, 'There is not any man of the Church of England but the same man is a member of the commonwealth, nor a member of the commonwealth which is not also a member of the Church of England'. The question was how this unity was to be restored: in what form episcopacy would be tolerable, what changes were necessary in the Prayer Book, how Separatists, often men of piety and learning, might be brought back into the Church, what fiscal arrangements would give the Crown an adequate revenue without the risk of absolutism, how to restrain the Commons from upsetting the constitutional balance, what foreign and colonial policies would bring best advantage to the merchants, how much regulation was necessary to assist the expansion of the economy. These were practical problems capable of practical solution, but in the wasted months of suspicion and tactical sparring no constructive attempt was made to deal with them. If now a physical clash of arms was necessary to clear the air, both sides intended that it should be brief, a mere prelude to negotiation. Charles, if he had won, might have executed some traitors, but no one would have tried to recover for him the powers he had used before 1640.

It is not possible here to pursue the war in any detail. Edward Hyde said that 'the number of those who desired to sit still was greater than of those who desired to engage in either party'. The war was a tiny affair, with not more than 140,000 in arms in four years. Towns and county associations thought only of local defence and were ready to come to terms with the party that was nearest or would inconvenience them least. Carmarthen was of no great importance but its behaviour was typical: it hopefully changed sides three times between October 1645 and the following July. Apart from isolated explosions of passion, the war was conducted with little of the savagery and strength-sapping guerrilla fighting of the Thirty Years War.

Charles's best hope of winning lay in the number of his enemies who did not want him to lose, but in the military sense he needed to strike a decisive blow immediately and his chances disappeared with the failure of his three-pronged advance on London in 1643. In Aubrey's view the decision to besiege Gloucester, taken on the advice of Falkland, was 'the procatarctique cause of his ruin'. But he would not have been Charles if he had not contributed to his own defeat through the inconsistency of his aims, interference with commanders in the field (notably with Rupert at Turnham Green), the intrigues of the exiled court at Oxford and the refusal to allow promotion on military merit. Rupert's impulsive methods were better suited to continental warfare on a larger terrain, and with Parliament holding the inner lines of communication royalist strategy wasted manpower on the garrisoning of outlying towns. The odds were hopeless once the initial impetus was spent. The buccaneering Earl of Warwick brought the navy to Parliament and sealed the ports through which Charles hoped to bring reinforcements. London, twelve times larger than any provincial city, was the centre of the country's wealth and trade, with its own arsenal, access to the Wealden iron, and a citizen militia that intervened decisively at Turnham Green and Gloucester. The possession of London enabled Parliament to take over the administrative machinery and to pay their armies through a centralised financial system that had never been available to the Crown. They imposed a new excise tax, collected the customs and levied monthly assessments on the counties, and there was no question of not paying the dues when soldiers came to collect them. Charles had none of these advantages, but he stubbornly prolonged the war until 1646, nourishing himself on fatuous hopes of deliverance by Montrose's Highlanders, the Irish Catholics or the foreign aid the Queen was always going to send from the Continent.

The war saw the end of Pym, who died in 1643 shortly after sending Sir Harry Vane to form the Solemn League and Covenant with the Scots. Although militarily useful, this was another disastrous piece of instant politics because it committed Parliament to terms which after the war were very inconvenient. Religion was to be prescribed 'according to the Word of God, and the example of the best Reformed Churches', and an assembly at Westminster would hammer out the details. So the price of victory was to be a Presbyterian order for which, except briefly as a gage of battle in the 1570s, the country had never shown any affection. It was a typically unfortunate legacy from Pym and his sterile talent for political manipulation. It had always been his aim to exploit religious passions when they suited his purposes and to keep them out of sight when they might be inconvenient. The failure of this policy at certain critical times suggests the continuing importance of the religious motive.

The war also saw the rise of Cromwell, craggy and carbuncular, a man in middle age before his life found a real purpose. He found it among the 'plain russet-coated captains' of the Eastern Association, 'such men as had the fear of God before them, and made some conscience of what they did'. When in the cause of military efficiency he refused to force his men to take the oath to the Covenant which Parliament had prescribed, religious toleration was beginning for the first time to become a serious issue. Events seemed to justify him, because Marston Moor (1644) 'had all the evidence of an absolute victory obtained by the Lord's blessing upon the godly party principally', the godly party being the sectaries who were impatient of religious prescription. Religious freedom was not the thing first contested for, he was to say later, although God 'brought it to that issue at the last'. For the moment he was inspired by his victories, in which he saw the clear hand of Providence, to bring a new attitude to the conduct of the war. To sustain the morale of their troops Parliament had attached to all the regiments zealous Puritan preachers, men like Stephen Marshall, an Essex vicar whom Clarendon regarded as one of the most influential men of the period. These preachers taught the soldiers that the defeat of the King would be the dawn of a new society revitalised by spiritual ideals, which was not at all the object of officers who came from a different social level. The commander-in-chief was the Earl of Essex, a dull, lugubrious man who included a coffin in his military baggage. If Cromwell met the King on the battlefield, he would draw his pistol 'as at any other private person', but Essex and Manchester were reluctant to 'beat the King too much'. Their object was to avoid clashing with his main army and to wear him down by capturing his garrisons and skirmishing with his reserves; and they had accepted the Covenant not through any love of Presbyterianism but because it provided a cut-and-dried solution of a difficult problem and would preserve 'the golden reins of discipline' necessary to the maintenance of the established order. Early in 1645 they were trying to negotiate with the King at Uxbridge when Cromwell accused them in the Commons of 'backwardness to fight'. The Self-Denying Ordinance decreed that all who had been appointed to military commands by the present Parliament should relinquish them within forty days, although they might be reappointed, as Cromwell himself and Fairfax immediately were. This move also had the support of the professionals who had formerly been fighting on the Continent and were not accustomed to engaging in wars where victory was not the prime objective. At the same time plans were laid for the creation of the New Model, the first English professional army, which was to be put under a unified command and made available for service in any part of the country. After early teething troubles a proper training and discipline were imposed, payment was regular, and with the advantage of mobility the New Model had finished the war by the summer of 1646.

It may be more difficult to disband a successful army than to reconcile a defeated one. The Self-Denying Ordinance had shown a diversity of aim that was bound to complicate the post-war settlement; and although not all the rough-neck conscripts of the New Model were men of high crusading purpose, the habit of victory had united the army in the possession of God's special favour. Democratic promotion from the ranks had weakened social barriers, and their chaplains had addressed them constantly on the redemptive tasks that lay ahead. Parliament, on the other hand, had had only one specific war aim, to bring Charles to the conference table, and this was still their only programme in time of peace, except that they now had a religious commitment to the Scots.

A common simplification of this period describes Parliament as Presbyterian and the army as Independent, but neither this nor any other simple formula, such as conservative against radical, will wholly fit the facts. As in 1641–2, there was the constant pull of other interests, local or personal, family or class; and the attitude of groups and individuals was always changing with events. Parliament was never wholly Presbyterian, or not in the Scottish sense. The Westminster Assembly met first in July 1643, before the Covenant was signed, to debate the religious reformation promised in the Grand Remonstrance, and even when the Scots commissioners were added, progress was slow. The Covenant stipulated that reform should be 'according to the Word of God', a crafty move which secured the temporary allegiance of Cromwell and many others who would not have said that the Presbyterian system was unassailably scriptural. Thus it was possible for the uncommitted Presbyterians in the Assembly, including a majority of the lay members, to protract the discussions and to insist at every stage on lay control of the congregations and the provincial and national synods. In the fullness of time the Assembly produced a Directory of Public Worship to supersede the Prayer Book, proclaimed by ordinance in January 1645, and the Westminster Confession, a standard formulary of Calvinist doctrine, completed by the end of 1646. But despite the alarming spread of sectarianism in London and the army, little was done to enforce public observance of these changes. It was not until October 1646 that episcopacy was formally abolished, although in practice the bishops had ceased to function, and the consecration of Thomas Howell at Bristol in 1644 was the last for sixteen years. Parliament was clearly determined to prevent the Presbyterians from establishing a new form of clerical despotism.

Baillie, one of the Scottish commissioners, regarded the Self-Denying Ordinance as a conspiracy to frustrate true religion, and the Independents in the Assembly and in the Commons obstructed the reformers' programme. In its 'classical' form, which had considerable support among the smaller gentry like Cromwell himself, Independency was not a separatist movement. It has been described as 'decentralised Calvinism', consisting of a loose federation of autonomous congregations within a national Church. Because the Church contained the reprobate as well as the elect, the magistrate was required to suppress profanity and 'insolent opposition to truth'. But he exercised only 'a defensive power for religion', since each congregation had the power to direct its own discipline and worship without interference from synods or higher officials. Saltmarsh, a chaplain in the New Model, claimed that 'all spiritual government is here, and not in any power foreign or extrinsical to the congregation, or authoritative', but he warned congregations to bind themselves in brotherly communion without assuming 'any power of infallibility to each other . . . for another's evidence is as dark to me as mine to him'. The anonymous *Ancient Bounds* (1645) argued similarly that any restraint on opinion, although intended for the correction of error, 'through the unskilfulness of man may fall upon the truth'. Thus the Independents' demand for religious toleration was not just provoked by the fear of persecution from above or by sectarian agitation in the ranks below. It was always implicit in their attitude to higher authority, and indeed some variety of opinion and practice was in the long run an inevitable consequence of the individualist nature of Puritan inspiration.

Independent orthodoxy therefore shaded into the more radical views of the 'sect-type' Puritanism which flourished with the relaxing of ecclesiastical discipline and the intoxication of military success. For Cromwell the heart of the Christian faith was personal religious experience, and he defended toleration so that it should not be imperilled, but the passionate conviction of the sects was in many ways an embarrassment. Inheriting the separatism of Browne and Barrow, they believed that a true Church consisted only of the elect; and although they expected the State to protect them, they admitted no connection with a national Church or even with society. They made a distinction between 'natural' unregenerate man, who needed the discipline of positive law, and man in grace, for whom the social order was trivial. The only freedom they sought was in the service of God, the only equality that which recognises the superiority of the elect over other men and protects their spiritual privileges. The devout sectaries valued religious experience above everything else and found in it a means of salvation that might be as effective as predestined grace. For many of them this experience was so intense that they stood aside from the true Calvinist mission to reform society and awaited the Second Coming for which a victorious war had prepared the way.

In a confused situation the political and social radicalism of the Levellers brought a different challenge to the traditional assumptions of society. To be a Leveller, however secular, was also to have radical ideas in religion, and the different aims of radicalism are hard to distinguish. Richard Overton, a cobbler who abandoned his last and founded a sect called the Soul Sleepers, was by 1646 a political Leveller, but he had no doubts about the sovereignty of the illuminated spiritual judgment [23]. But the Levellers were not in the least other-worldly, and in the debates of the army at Reading and Putney, and in John Lilburne's four issues of the Agreement of the People, they declared the social policies for which, in their view, the war had been fought. 'Levelling' had an ancestry that reached back to the 'Commonwealth' writers of the sixteenth century, Jack Cade, the Peasants' Revolt, and the time-honoured persuasion that there were no privileged landowners around when Adam dug the garden patch and Eve was knitting for the little ones. So the aristocracy were only the heirs of William the Conqueror's invading officers, and Magna Carta, which confirmed their unwarrantable privileges, bore the scars of an intolerable bondage. An essential in everyone's eyes was that the Long Parliament, or what remained of it, should dissolve itself, and the Levellers' programme included a wide extension of the franchise (though not to wage-earners, most of the radicals being yeoman farmers and small traders), abolition of the Lords, election of JPs, biennial parliaments and various legal reforms. The practical implications were not worked out, and Shakespeare had already said much of it in Act IV of *2 Henry VI*. The problem for Ireton, Cromwell and the other officers was that they sympathised with the spirit of these demands, and they wrestled long and earnestly with the army 'agitators' even while—to their own discredit among the radicals—they were trying to negotiate a durable settlement with the King. The more drastic reforms represented only the views of an articulate minority, and Cromwell argued that these 'carnal reasonings' would lead to confusion and endanger what had been won. The Englishman's birthright, Ireton said, was 'air and place and ground and the freedom of the highways and other things'. But when authority was in question, he would 'have an eye to property' and reserve it in the traditional way to those with 'a permanent fixed interest in this kingdom'. Religious idealism likewise might lose all if it overturned an ancient system deeply embedded in the social structure, and were not the privileges of the saints in conflict with other men's notions of popular rights? By November 1647 the officers had more or less asserted their authority when the King escaped and made an alliance with the Scots to renew the war. This converted the officers to the view that Charles must die, but at the Whitehall debates in December 1648 they were still urging the dangers of separatism.

In this tumultuous period the difficulties of Parliament have not always been appreciated. At least they tried to bring about a 'politique' settlement that the vast majority of a war-weary nation desired, and a Presbyterian solution of the religious problem had proved workable elsewhere. England had one of the few reformed Churches that had never tried it. There was even a rational explanation for the attempt to ship the army to Ireland, where there was still God's work to be done, before their arrears of pay had been made up. After years of confiscations and crippling taxation Parliament would have had to find some £330,000 for this purpose. But the grievance of the unpaid conscript was thereby linked with the aspirations of sectary and Leveller, and in a Declaration from St Albans in June 1647 the army reminded Parliament that they were no mercenary body and that they had a right to be heard in the settlement of the kingdom [24]. Charles held the key to the situation because so far only a handful of radicals would have contemplated a settlement without him, but he fatuously believed that he would better the final terms if he prevaricated long enough. At the end of the war he had surrendered to the Scots, confident in the royalism the Covenanters always professed. To his Queen, a daughter of Henry IV, England was worth a Covenant, but the talks foundered on religion and Charles was handed over to Parliament. Fearing that he might accept the terms which Parliament had submitted to him at Newcastle, the army brought him to the camp at Newmarket (June 1647) and offered him Ireton's Heads of the Proposals, the most moderate and constructive of the schemes suggested at this time. There was to be no coercive power in religion, and restraints were proposed on Parliament as well as on the Crown. But it was too comprehensive to be acceptable to any party, and after Charles and Parliament had both rejected it he escaped—or was allowed to escape—to the Isle of Wight, where in December he concluded the

Engagement with the Scots. In return for three years of Presbyterianism they would crush the sects and force the army to disband.

Scattered royalist risings had been suppressed before a half-hearted Scottish army crossed the border in the summer. In a long, straggling battle between Preston and Warrington, Cromwell achieved one of the greatest of his victories, and his menacing dispatch from the field warned Parliament not to misuse it [25]. But they at once resumed negotiations with the King, and in the Remonstrance of the Army (November 1648) Ireton, now disillusioned and ruthless, accepted the Levelling doctrine of popular sovereignty and demanded the removal of the Man of Blood. Pride's Purge ejected the last of the irreconcilable Presbyterians and reduced the Long Parliament to a rump of some fifty time-servers and careerists in whose name a court was set up to try the King.

So Puritanism came to the great purple act. Despite the presence of secular motives, only the Puritans would have done it this way, conceiving it as a ritual expiation, an act performed not in a corner but in the sight of all men, to show that earthly authority is 'but dross and dung in comparison with Christ'. But it turned into black comedy, with President Bradshaw in his shot-proof hat, which can be seen in the Ashmolean Museum in Oxford, and Cromwell in a mood of ghastly facetiousness throwing cushions and inking men's faces as he hawked the warrant of death, the executioners in false beards and wigs. Charles defeated his enemies by refusing to defend himself before a court which differed only in its pompous externals from a drumhead court martial. Since 1642 he had steadily refused to compromise his remaining prerogatives, and if a king could be treated thus, no man was safe from a military junta that was subverting law and the constitution. 'I am not suffered for to speak. Expect what justice other people will have.' Promptly on his execution the emotive subtleties of *Eikon Basilike* challenged even the Puritans' special prerogative of the appeal to Heaven.

3

The Single Person

When virtue's steely bones
Look bleak i' th' cold wind.
ALL'S WELL THAT ENDS WELL I i 114

The Interregnum had little prospect of being anything else. The Rump declared the abolition of monarchy and the House of Lords, and when it was itself dissolved by force in 1653, nothing remained of traditionally-constituted authority. Any future Parliament would only be by permission of the army, which had already diminished the status of the Commons by successive purges during 1647. After the brief 'Barebones' experiment, the new constitution-making simply moved back towards the old system. An upper house was restored, 'His Highness' the Protector was virtually King and could nominate his successor, and despite further purgings a Commons dominated by landed gentry asserted their ancient rights against the executive. In constitutional terms there had almost been a 'restoration' before 1660. The army itself was socially conservative after the officers had broken the short-lived radical alliance of 1648 by executing the ringleaders of a mutiny at Burford in May 1649 and ending the influence of the agitators. Levelling ideas persisted in many areas, and within a month of the King's execution Lilburne, promoter of the Agreement of the People, was petitioning the Rump on England's 'new chains'. But Lilburne was regarded by Cromwell much as he had been regarded by Laud, and the Levellers, who had expected to be architects of the future, shrank into a noisy insignificance. The revolution had lost its revolutionary impetus.

The same thing happened in religion. Puritans ceased to be an active force for the transformation of society when Parliament was unable, or partly unwilling, to translate the work of the Westminster Assembly into a national system. This was the end of the attempt to build a Puritan Church of England. The Rump's Engagement (1649–50), which required of all males over the age of 18 a declaration of loyalty to 'the Commonwealth of England as it is now established, without a King or House of Lords', did not demand subscription to the Covenant. In theory, the Directory of Public Worship was still in force and use of the Prayer Book was forbidden (and an ordinance in November 1655 did again specifically forbid it); in theory, tithe and lay patronage were to be abolished. However, the practice was almost as disorderly and various as it had ever been, with the Anglicans, now the undercover party, worshipping privately and still recruiting to the ministry although there was no official machinery of ordination. It is said that Presbyterians and Independents amicably shared their churches, and rather than sanction the extravagances of the sects, propertied Independents were willing to serve as Presbyterian elders or present their clergy to impropriated benefices. 'Are they not choked with manors?' one critic asked, and Clement Walker, a Somerset Presbyterian ejected by Colonel Pride, thought that 'all the cheating, covetous, ambitious persons of the land' were climbing on the band-wagon in the name of godliness. This was a natural reaction but not generally accurate. Jeremy Taylor, who continued to recite the Anglican office from memory, was nearer the mark when he said that 'the worship of God was left to chance, indeliberation and a petulant fancy'.

With the Presbyterian failure and the proliferation of the sects, Puritanism had lost its direction. Truth was no longer to be found in the old Calvinist certainties but in the private illumination of those who felt themselves to be in exultant communion with God. These men were inward-looking, intent upon their own saintliness and the saintliness of their congregations; they did not believe, as their fathers had, that it was possible to win the whole kingdom for God, and they were almost passive as they awaited the Second Coming which the Fifth Monarchists had fixed for 1656 and their brethren for a date less precise but certainly imminent. A great change had come over Puritanism when the elect merely expected society to protect them instead of dedicating themselves to change. It is true that the Rump and Cromwell's Major-Generals continued the Long Parliament's policy of moral and social prohibition. The theatres had been closed, Sabbath observance narrowed to the point of obsession, adultery made a capital offence, Christmas abolished [26] and mince pies declared an idolatrous indulgence. This dreary work continued, but it was losing much of its earlier conviction. Cromwell's heart was never in these outward forms of piety. He feared only that assemblies for public recreation would be a cover for conspiracy and riot.

Wenceslas Hollar, an engraver from Prague who later prepared a valuable map of London after the Great Fire, told Aubrey that on his return from exile in 1652 he 'found the countenances of the people all changed, melancholy, spiteful, as if bewitched'. Through surfeit of their function, and the relentless stridency of their pulpit style, even the popular preachers were losing acceptance. Evelyn congratulated himself on coming upon an Independent minister who 'ordinarily preached sound doctrine, and was a peaceable man, which was an extraordinary felicity in this age'. Dorothy Osborne's reception of the celebrated Stephen Marshall anticipated by a hundred years Horace Walpole's distaste for Wesley's 'ugly enthusiasm', but the intellectual tide was already on the turn [27]. The Church had its own models of piety in the learning and devotion of the Caroline divines or Ferrar's community at Little Gidding or the sweetness of George Herbert's life at Bemerton. At Cambridge, even during the years of the Protectorate, the Cambridge Platonists were opening the windows in a university that had become as obscurantist as Valladolid. All but Henry More were Emmanuel men and therefore started from a Puritan position, but they held that spiritual truth was discoverable by reason and man's inward apprehension, not by the tyrannies of dogma. In a sermon preached before the Commons at the end of the war Ralph Cudworth, a Cambridge philosopher, said that 'it is another mistake we have of God, by shaping Him according to the model of ourselves, when we make Him nothing but a blind, dark, impetuous self-will running through the world'. A steady weakening of Puritan confidence helped to accomplish a bloodless Restoration.

The decade bears the personal mark of the wrestling Jacob who presided over it. Cromwell was sure that finally it would not matter 'what men will make of these actings', but he damaged the Puritan cause by narrowing the basis on which it had formerly stood. In the flush of further victories he came to identify true religion with the men who had shared them, until it became difficult for a civilian to pass through the eye of this particular needle. In 1649 he was in Ireland, where the barbarities at Drogheda and Wexford were 'seals of God's approbation of your great change of government'. Thus God 'breaks the enemies of His Church in pieces'. It is idle to pretend that Cromwell did not thrive on the smell of sacrifice. His butcheries did not have the justification of military necessity, as Ormonde's field army had already been defeated at Rathmines, and his only practical excuse might be that he was in a hurry because his army was needed in Scotland. He left Ireton to consummate the policy that envenomed Ireland for centuries. In a so-called plantation scheme the natives were pushed westward into infertile Connaught, and two-thirds of the land came into the possession of soldiers, politicians and speculators.

In Scotland the future Charles II had revived the Royalist–Presbyterian alliance by accepting the Covenant. Fairfax resigned rather than invade the sister kingdom, and for the first time Cromwell was in supreme command of the Rumping army. He had never liked the Scots or trusted them. His dispatch after Marston Moor discounted their contribution to a victory 'obtained by the Lord's blessing upon the godly party principally'. But they were brethren divided from the godly only by differences which should be mended by greater understanding, and he besought them 'in the bowels of Christ' to think it possible they might be mistaken. At Dunbar the Lord confirmed their error. Strategically outmanoeuvred before the battle, Cromwell was saved when the Covenanting clergy talked General Leslie into abandoning his superior position on the Lammermuirs, and within an hour the Scots had lost 3,000 killed and 10,000 prisoners (September 1650). 'Surely it's probable the Kirk has done their do.' Leslie raised another force, and rather than face a second winter campaign in 1651–2, Cromwell cut off Leslie in the Highlands and deliberately left the road into England open. Not for the last time, an invading Scottish army failed to win recruits in Lancashire and Wales, and the 'crowning mercy' was vouchsafed at Worcester on the anniversary of Dunbar.

The work of the Rump between 1649 and 1653 has been discredited by Cromwell's final demonstration against them. In the unprecedented circumstances they did well to govern at all. The Council of State and its subordinate committees raised money for Cromwell's campaigns and also for the naval operations which secured the allegiance of the West Indies settlements and chased Prince Rupert's royalist ships out of Ireland and across the Mediterranean into Toulon. They passed a Navigation Act (1651) and began a commercial war against the Dutch, who had captured much of the carrying-trade. They repressed the Levellers, the Diggers and other advocates of social revolution. But the cost was high in the disappointment of recent hopes, the confiscation of royalist and ecclesiastical property to pay expenses, the suppression of free speech and the enforcement of harsh penalties in arbitrary tribunals. Repeal of the laws enforcing church attendance encouraged the strange importunities of the sects, and a savage Blasphemy Act did little to restrain them. The Rump set up a Committee for the Propagation of the Gospel and toyed with John Owen's scheme for a national Church with toleration for nonconforming congregations, but they could not settle the religious problem, and when they began to propose a reduction in the forces as a desirable economy the army demanded reform on the lines of their Declaration of 1647 and the subsequent Heads of the Proposals.

The crux of the dispute came to be the Rump's own existence, as for years the army had been seeking the dissolution of the Long Parliament and a new election on a reformed franchise. The Rump were realistic enough to see that an election would produce a conservative reaction hostile to the whole regime, a sombre truth which Cromwell was presently to discover for himself. They accordingly proposed that the members should continue to sit for the rest of their lives and be allowed to co-opt others of whom they approved. When Cromwell dissolved them with a file of musketeers, blending appeals to Heaven with coarse abuse of the members, it seemed that Charles had died for Parliament as well as for the Crown.

The Barebones Parliament was only a Parliament at all because the members so decreed themselves. It was intended to be a nominated assembly to fill the gap while the constitution was temporarily suspended. The 140 members, of whom eleven represented Scotland and Ireland, were selected by the officers from lists of 'divers persons fearing God, and of approved fidelity and honesty' submitted by the Independent congregations. At their meeting Cromwell declared that he 'never looked to see such a day as this—it may be, nor you either—when Jesus Christ should be so owned as He is, at this day and in this work. . . . Indeed, I do think somewhat is at the door'. Although Clarendon took a less apocalyptic view of their performance [28], this was in a sense the climax of the Puritan movement, when men were summoned not because they had property or influence but because they were saintly men fearing God. In five months of feverish activity the enthusiasts among them abolished Chancery, established civil marriage, attacked tithes and lay patronage and proposed to re-write the laws within 'the bigness of a pocket-book'. Lambert and the moderates in the assembly got up early one morning and dissolved it (December 1653).

'The issue was not answerable to the simplicity and honesty of the design.' Cromwell's religious ideals were always in conflict with the conservative instincts of a squire who believed in subordination and degree. 'A nobleman, a gentleman, a yeoman: the distinction of these: that is a good interest of the nation, and a great one.' The creed of the Levellers was like the crackling of thorns under a pot, and he would have liked to restore the institutions he had destroyed, subject always to the interests of 'God's people', those that were as the apple of His eye. He would not therefore accept any settlement without a guarantee of religious toleration, and it was the continuing dilemma of the Protectorate that toleration—'spiritual whoredom' to an orthodox Puritan like Thomas Case—could only be upheld by force. Cromwell had to 'disarm the nine and put the sword in the tenth man's hand', and this hated dependence on military rule stood in the way of a constitutional settlement. After the failure of the Saints in 1653 and the symbolic cashiering of General Harrison, a fanatical Fifth Monarchist, Cromwell looked increasingly to the 'ancient interests' of the kingdom, but the Protectorate was doomed to progressive anti-climax. No ruler is better than the amount of confidence reposed in him. Cromwell failed to reconcile the royalists, whom he harassed with renewed confiscations, and he was hated by republicans, Levellers, parliamentarians and many of his old comrades whose hopes he had disappointed [29]. In his pamphlet, *King Richard III Revived*, Prynne decided that he had been better governed under Charles I.

The Instrument of Government (1653), drawn up by Lambert and the officers, divided power between a Single Person and a Council of fifteen, all nominated for life, and a single-chamber Parliament to be elected on a system which vastly increased the county representation at the expense of the boroughs and gave the vote to men with property worth £200 a year in place of the forty-shilling freeholder. Parliament was not to meet until 3 September 1654, the anniversary of Dunbar and Worcester, even though it happened to be a Sunday. In the meantime Cromwell made it clear that in spite of earlier promises he did not intend to abolish tithe and patronage, nor even lay impropriations, until a better system had been devised. He took refuge in a clumsy compromise by setting up a commission of Triers, with lay representatives, to test the fitness of candidates presented to lectureships and livings, and Ejectors to remove clergy and teachers found, in their opinion, to be 'scandalous, ignorant and insufficient'. Thus bad men could not fill benefices with bad men, and only ministers of 'holy and unblameable conversation' would be able to handle the emoluments of the Church. This might fulfil the old Puritan demand for a pious and learned ministry, but a Fifth Monarchist, John Rogers, exposed the flaw when he asked who made the Triers judges of grace. The gentry merely saw an interference with the rights of property, and it was questionable whether this system was any improvement on the old traditional one of episcopal visitation and censure in the ecclesiastical courts. Once again the revolution was veering back to established methods.

The first Protectorate Parliament (1654–5) similarly revived the old techniques of opposition, and it was found that the Instrument, which had intended to balance the powers of legislature and executive, had left the sword as the only arbiter if they should fail to agree. Even after the customary purge a House packed with independently-minded country gentlemen criticised the constitution under which they sat, notably the granting to the Protector of a substantial income not subject to parliamentary control. Self-justification was the keynote in Cromwell's speech when he reproachfully dissolved them after the minimum statutory period, and on the pretext of the dangers of royalist conspiracy he parcelled the country into eleven districts under Major-Generals. They were to raise and train a civilian militia, as Cromwell was hoping to save money by reducing the regular army, and their own expenses were met by a decimation tax on royalist estates. At least this was a logical system because it supplied the centralised administration, properly financed, which the Crown had sought in vain. The Major-Generals were *intendants* who took over the work of the prerogative courts, the church courts, the Justices of the Peace and the Presbyterian elders. With a special instruction to 'promote virtue', they also carried out the moral programme of Puritanism by enforcing the vice laws with stern evangelist zeal, but the gentry were aghast at the usurpation of their rights and privileges, and the decimation was particularly disturbing because it was an unparliamentary tax.

Cromwell finally withdrew the Major-Generals, with some hypocritical criticism of their actions, because he needed Parliament's financial help with his foreign policy. Perhaps the greatest achievement of the Interregnum was the foundation of a professional navy, a sea-going equivalent of the New Model in which with typical regicide pedantry the admirals were called Generals-at-Sea. Some 200 new ships were launched, making the navy no longer dependent on conscripted merchantmen; pay, food and discipline were improved, and a more centralised command permitted the development of new tactics. Robert Blake, who had defended Bristol and Taunton against the King, went on to crush the royalist resistance at sea, while Richard Deane, commander of the Roundhead artillery at Naseby, modernised naval administration. In the First Dutch War (1652–4) the English challenged and contained the previous masters of the sea, avenged at last the Amboyna massacre of 1623 and opened vast imperial possibilities.

Here was a formidable instrument to Cromwell's hand, but it is difficult to find a controlling pattern in a policy in which national, economic, party, religious and imperialist interests battled for possession of his mind. At one time he would have a Puritan crusade, because 'God's interest in the world is more extensive than all the people of these three nations. God has brought us hither to consider the work we may do in the world as well as at home'. He had visions of launching the warlike Charles X against the Empire as Richelieu had once launched Gustavus Adolphus, but the internal rivalry of the Scandinavian powers defeated his attempt to combine them for a Protestant crusade, and he had to be content with securing solid commercial advantages in the Baltic. Overtures to Spain broke down on the Spanish refusal to cede Dunkirk, captured from France in 1652, or to admit English merchants to the South American trade: whereupon Cromwell told Parliament that 'truly your great enemy is the Spaniard. He is naturally so, by reason of that enmity that is in him against whatsoever is of God.' To his Council he said that 'Providence seemed to lead us, having 160 ships swimming; most of Europe our enemies'. Unpopular at home, he took the advice of the Machiavellian Bolingbroke to 'busy giddy minds with foreign quarrels'. The legend of *Albion perfide* may have begun with Cromwell. Without a formal declaration of war he landed an ill-found expedition on Hispaniola, the largest of the Caribbean islands. While the men died of thirst and dysentery, Colonel Venables succeeded in being twice ambushed on the same spot. The expedition was Tudor in its improvisation and its lack of precise objectives, and Cromwell punished it with Tudor penalties, Venables and Admiral Penn being imprisoned in the Tower. The importance of the incidental capture of Jamaica (1655) was not immediately appreciated, and Cromwell, sensitive to the disapproval of the City financiers, humbly concluded that 'we have provoked the Lord; and it is good for us to know and to be abased for the same'.

When a new Parliament was summoned in September 1656 the Major-Generals failed so badly in their attempt to influence the elections that a hundred members had to be excluded before the House assembled. Parliament at once refused to sanction a continuance of the decimation tax, and the savage punishment of James Nayler, a Quaker who rode into Bristol on an ass claiming to be Christ, was designed as a warning to Cromwell on the dangers of religious toleration. The Humble Petition and Advice (1657), which proposed to restore monarchy and an upper house, did not represent a conscious royalist reaction. It aimed to establish a hereditary succession for fear of the anarchy that might follow the Protector's death, but the purpose was to reduce Cromwell's powers, not extend them. Monarchy was known to the constitution and could be brought within the rule of law, whereas the Protectorate seemed to make its own laws. Cromwell would have liked to accept an office that would have brought him nearer to the settlement that he desired, and it was not the self-seeking of the officers that deterred him. He surrendered finally to the testimony of the common soldiers, 'God's people' with whom he had fought and won his battles for a higher purpose than an earthly crown. It was an agonising decision and a wrong one, as the nearer the Protectorate came to the old constitution, the less justification it had for its own existence. Genuine royalists and republicans were still irreconcilable, and with the elevation of many of Cromwell's most active supporters to the Other House the amended constitution was an immediate failure. In February 1658 he dispersed Parliament for the last time [30].

Before he died, followed to the last by his obsession about anniversaries, Cromwell saw his Ironsides earn the respect of the great Turenne at the Battle of the Dunes, where they won Dunkirk, a prize operationally too expensive to be worth keeping. A sullen nation was not to be dazzled by this conquest, any more than it had earlier been dazzled by Stayner's capture of a Spanish treasure-fleet or Blake's last great victory off Santa Cruz. Although, with almost unlimited opportunities for taxation, the Protectorate had raised revenues four times as great as Charles I's, it had never been solvent, and just as Charles had done it had lost the confidence of the City. That was its practical failure. It had also helped to reduce Puritanism from a great reforming movement to the survival under military protection of a small and precocious *élite*, an outcome that possibly had been implicit all the time in the very nature of its inspiration. Through all the agglutinations of his speech and thought and his many eloquent assaults on the constitution, Cromwell had been loyal to the English interest as it presented itself to a conservative Elizabethan squire, but this loyalty had been too seldom reconcilable with the semi-mystical faith of a man who walked consciously in the imputed righteousness of Christ and followed the guidance of Providences 'so clear and so unclouded' that it would have been 'very atheism' to resist them.

In one of his not infrequent moods of disillusion at men's failure to accept his vision of their destiny Cromwell confessed that 'I could not tell what my business was . . . save comparing myself to a good constable set to keep the peace of the parish'. That at least he was, and his peace collapsed as soon as he was gone. He had not bequeathed a settled constitution, and after a few weeks of deceptive calm the soldiers were again in conflict with the civil power. Yet another Protectorate Parliament was dissolved by force, Richard Cromwell resigned his unwelcome office and went abroad, and the recall of the Rump soon brought Parliament and army to the deadlock of 1647, now with no King to be made the scapegoat of their failure to agree. Then Monk marched in from Scotland, and acting with a truly Tudor moderation and sagacity that had not been seen in England for sixty years, he patiently sensed the will of the nation before negotiating the restoration of the King.

EPILOGUE

Is all your strict preciseness come to this?

I HENRY VI, V iv 67

The settlement at the Restoration intended to resume the relationship of Crown and Parliament that had been interrupted after the reforms of 1641. The prerogative courts were not revived, the Privy Council lost its criminal jurisdiction, ship-money and other unparliamentary sources of revenue were forbidden and the King had to summon Parliament at least once in three years. On the other hand, the issues in dispute in 1641 were settled in favour of the Crown, which might still appoint ministers, control the militia, direct foreign policy and exercise supremacy in religion. In return for the permanent surrender of wardship, purveyance and feudal tenures, already abolished in 1646, the Crown was granted a fixed annual revenue of £1,200,000; and the bishops were restored to the House of Lords and allowed to revive their courts, although they failed in a bid to recover High Commission too. This conservative settlement was chiefly the work of Clarendon, who saw no reason to depart from the Elizabethan principles embodied in it, but he had the support of a nation sceptical of Utopian solutions that led either to social chaos or to military despotism. The settlement upheld the rule of law and what Clarendon called 'the good old frame of government', and it was not only Anglicans who welcomed the restoration of the Church as a bulwark of stability and order. 'No bishop, no king' had its obvious corollary in 'no parson, no squire'.

But in practice it was impossible to pretend that twenty violent years had simply not occurred, and Clarendon himself was one of the earliest victims of an old man's misjudgment. Ever since Pym had set up an emergency system to run the war for Parliament in 1642, the country had governed itself through a network of committees that had superseded for ever the agencies of the aristocracy and the king; not even the Justices of the Peace fully recovered their former authority. On a larger scale this resembled the bureaucratic revolution carried out by Thomas Cromwell in the reign of Henry VIII, and England now had something like a professional civil service able to maintain an efficient administration in times of political upheaval.

There was social and economic change as well. Economic regulation continued through the Navigation Act, the only significant survival of the legislative activity of the Interregnum and itself only a development of older policies. The Second Dutch War (1665–7) was instigated by the Royal African Company in a search for foreign bases, and the Commonwealth navy was engaged in the conscious creation of an imperial trading unit from which foreigners, particularly the Dutch, were to be excluded. By the designation of 'enumerated articles' England became an entrepôt for the re-export of colonial produce and manufactures, and with increasing diversification in mining and a more sophisticated agriculture, the cloth trade lost its old preponderance in the economy. Internally, on the other hand, the policy of economic regulation for the common social good had disappeared with the weakening of the Crown's authority. The abolition of feudal tenures established a mass of freeholders who could do as they liked with their land, dictate rents and leases and gradually extinguish the copyholder. Industry likewise was freed from the restraints of the apprenticeship laws and the former controls on quality, wages and prices. The prevailing temper was evident in the Act of Settlement (1662), which virtually revived mediaeval villeinage by removing to their place of 'legal settlement' landless men who might be chargeable on the rates of other parishes.

The royal prerogative in foreign policy became meaningless since in normal times policy would be dictated by commercial interests, and Charles II would not have made any progress with his Francophile designs in the early 'seventies if he had not shrewdly calculated them to coincide with the merchants' readiness to strike a final blow at Holland. The Crown's fixed revenue always fell about a quarter of a million short of the sum Parliament had intended, and in 1665 they insisted on controlling the expenditure of additional supply. The King was therefore unable to pursue an independent policy unless he could either get subsidies from abroad or, by means of bribery and patronage, win sufficient support in the Commons. Finally, the royal supremacy in religion immediately proved to be a parliamentary supremacy when Charles's desire for a comprehensive settlement was defeated by the Clarendon Code.

At Breda Charles had promised, subject to Parliament's approval, a 'liberty to tender consciences', and in a public declaration he proposed a compromise similar to Bishop Ussher's scheme that had been debated in the Lords in 1641. The penal laws should be relaxed, ceremonial modified and the authority of the bishops limited by synods of presbyters. The

Presbyterians, innocent of the extravagances of the sects, assumed that they would be included in any settlement of religion, and they made the mistake of asking too much, reviving all the Puritan demands about vestments and outward observances. The Convention dispersed without making any proposals, leaving a settlement to a conference of Anglican and Puritan divines which the King called at the Savoy in 1661 to consult on alterations in the Prayer Book. Baxter, the leading spokesman for the Puritans, was so prolix, and the fundamental differences so wide, that the conference broke up in unspiritual acrimony. Meanwhile the elections to the Cavalier Parliament returned a phalanx of revengeful royalists, and the Clarendon Code (1662–5) excluded from their civil rights and the practice of their religion all who in conscience could not give 'unfeigned assent and consent to all and everything' contained in the Prayer Book of Queen Elizabeth. This was something entirely new. Laud had tried to gather all Protestants into a national Church, but now the law officially recognised the existence of dissent. There was, for what it was worth, a choice: men could remain in the Church or decide to leave it. At the same time the Church lost all claim to be independent of the State. These laws were made in Parliament for motives that were political and social rather than religious; and in 1664 the clergy surrendered their ancient right of taxing themselves in Convocation, which did not meet again until 1689, and in 1717 was suppressed for 135 years.

Bunyan, who spent twelve years in gaol under the Clarendon Code, wrote that at the Judgment it would not be asked, 'Did you believe? but, Were you doers, or talkers only?' For a hundred years the Puritans had been the most consistently active force in English society, never resting, even under persecution, in the service of God and the purification of man's daily life. They did not cause the English Revolution, because constitutional change must have resulted from the break with Rome, the growth of population, the development of science, the redistribution of wealth and other social factors. The genius of Calvin devised a new kind of religion for the fluid society of his time, and in England, as elsewhere, this religion helped to guide the course of revolution. In England the energising force of Puritanism, active in the Church, trade, politics, the law, administration and social life, combined and concentrated the other revolutionary causes. Revolutions are the stronger for a positive sense of mission. But in the end Puritanism failed to achieve its highest purposes. Some of the energy burnt itself out when it was gradually realised that the Puritan conception of freedom would never coincide with the nation's. Liberty was being championed by a partisan minority who refused it to everyone else. This was the élitist strain in Puritanism, the inalienable aristocracy of the elect, which could never be reconciled with class privilege or any realistic notion of popular rights.

Thus in many ways the Puritanism of the Restoration was ready to retreat. The less robust withdrew into their private obsessions and saw Antichrist under every paving-stone. The majority accepted their exclusion from a godless society and retired to practise true religion in the pious household and the sober decencies of trade. The Bible, so full of calls to action, taught also the virtues of resignation and promised rewards to those who served in that condition. The old Cromwellians, disbanded at last with their pay and a pardon, carried the habit of discipline into private life or, if they found it impossible to settle, went overseas to master the hard land and wrestle with the strange obduracy of the natives to religious conversion and economic exploitation. Puritanism did not lose its spirit under persecution. It simply domesticated itself to pursue its aims in a humbler, more gracious way and set about a new and silent revolution.

The Clarendon Code was only sporadic in its effects. Lay Puritanism had deep roots in the countryside, and there were now many 'conforming' Puritans who saw to it that the faithful should not be molested in their private worship. Orthodox royalists even began to fear that the loose application of the penal statutes was allowing the Jesuits to 'ensnare weaker judgments and draw them on to raise a new rebellion'. The Popish conspiracies of the 1670s, real and imaginary, tended to close the ranks when Protestantism was once again in danger, and it did not need Shaftesbury's dreary opportunism to convince the Puritans that they would receive better favour in calmer times. Charles II's belated conversion to strict Tory principles (1681–5) delayed the inevitable recognition, and the dissenters had then to resist a subtler approach than Shaftesbury's when James II tempted them with the promise of influence as well as freedom. Opportunities for advancement were offered with the Crown's revision of borough charters and the weeding out of officials who would not agree to the repeal of the Test Act. But Halifax, who viewed the Puritans' religion as 'a disease that hath seized upon their minds', persuaded them in his *Letter to a Dissenter* to mistrust a Catholic bearing gifts. 'The other day you were sons of Belial, now you are angels of light.'

The Puritans' reward for resisting James's seduction was the niggardly Toleration Act (1689), which granted most nonconformists freedom of worship but still excluded them from military command and public office. This was probably to their advantage because it left them free to exert their influence in other ways, through the example of personal piety and their unrivalled gift for communal worship; while for those who wished it, some participation in public life was made possible by the practice of 'occasional conformity', which the Tory extremists failed to prevent, and by Walpole's annual Indemnity Acts. Toleration was born eventually not of passion but of indifference, in a latitudinarian Church where Addison's Fox-hunter was unsurprised to learn that 'there is scarce a Presbyterian in the county, except the bishop'. In this more placid climate a closer reconciliation with the Church would have been possible if the Puritans had wished it, but there was little attraction for them in a body in which an archbishop could congratulate himself upon 'the wisdom of being religious'. They could serve God better by walking their chosen paths alone. They were still 'doers', diligent and thrifty, and most of the pioneers of the Industrial Revolution, the inventors, the great iron-masters, the entrepreneurs, were of nonconformist stock. Defeat in 1660 did not end the Puritan contribution to the development of modern Britain. It led to the Victorian Sunday, the servitude of those in menial occupations, the assumption that ethics, like over-eating, was for the successful; but Puritan thrift and energy and discipline led also to a period of great economic achievement and to the creation of an empire whose sons had the character to govern it responsibly.

EXTRACTS

1. On Being a Puritan
(page 10)

If any were grieved at the dishonour of the kingdom, or the griping of the poor, or the unjust oppressions of the subject, by a thousand ways invented to maintain the riots of the courtiers, and the swarms of needy Scots the King had brought in to devour like locusts the plenty of this land, he was a Puritan; if any, out of mere morality and civil honesty, discountenanced the abominations of those days, he was a Puritan, however he conformed to their superstitious worship; if any showed favour to any godly honest persons, kept them company, relieved them in want, or protected them against violent or unjust oppression, he was a Puritan; if any gentleman in his country maintained the good laws of the land, or stood up for any public interest, for good order or government, he was a Puritan; in short, all that crossed the views of the needy courtiers, the proud encroaching priests, the thievish projectors, the lewd nobility and gentry—whoever was zealous for God's glory or worship, could not endure blasphemous oaths, ribald conversation, profane scoffs, Sabbath breaking, derision of the word of God, and the like—whoever could endure a sermon, modest habit or conversation, or anything good—all these were Puritans; and if Puritans, then enemies to the King and his government, seditious, factious hypocrites, ambitious disturbers of the public peace, and finally, the pest of the kingdom.

LUCY HUTCHINSON, *Memoirs of Colonel Hutchinson* (*c.* 1665)

(The passage refers to the reign of James I.)

2. God Almighty
(page 12)

1. God from eternity had predestinated some to life, some He hath reprobated to death.

2. The moving or efficient cause of predestination to life is not the prevision of faith, or of perseverance, or of good works, or of anything which may be in the persons predestinated, but only the will of the good pleasure of God.

3. Of the predestinated there is a fore-limited and certain number which can neither be diminished nor increased.

4. They who are not predestinated to salvation will be necessarily condemned on account of their sins. . .

9. It is not placed in the will or power of every man to be saved.

THE LAMBETH ARTICLES (1595)

3. Disordered Worship
(page 19)

Some say the service and prayers in the chancel, others in the body of the church; some say the same in a seat made in the church, some in the pulpit with their faces to the people; some keep precisely the order of the book, others intermeddle psalms in metre; some say in a surplice, others without a surplice; the table standeth in the body of the church in some places, in others it standeth in the chancel; in some places the table standeth altarwise, distant from the wall a yard, in some others in the middle of the chancel, north and south; in some places the table is joined, in others it standeth upon trestles; in some places the table hath a carpet, in others it hath not; administration of the Communion is done by some with surplice and cap, some with surplice alone, others with none; some with chalice, others with a Communion cup, others with a common cup; some with unleavened bread, some with leavened; some receive kneeling, others standing, others sitting; some baptise in a font, some in a basin; some sign with the sign of the cross, others sign not. Apparel—some with a square cap, some with a round cap, some with a button cap, some with a hat.

SUMMARY OF RETURNS FROM THE DIOCESES SUBMITTED TO WILLIAM CECIL IN 1564

4. Puritan Admonitions
(page 25)

May it therefore please your wisdoms to understand, we in England are
so far off from having a Church rightly reformed, according to the pre-
script of God's Word, that as yet we are not come to the outward face of
the same. For to speak of that wherein all consent and whereupon all
writers accord: the outward marks whereby a true Christian Church is
known are preaching the Word purely, ministering of the sacraments
sincerely, and ecclesiastical discipline which consisteth in admonition
and correction of faults severely...

FIELD AND WILCOX, *The First Admonition to the Parliament* (1572)

The life of the Word is the ministry of the same. The former treatises
therefore have rightly spoken against the bastard, idle and unpreaching
ministry of this Church...

You must repeal your statute or statutes whereby you have authorised
that ministry that now is, making your estate partly to consist of Lords
spiritual (as you call them), and making one minister higher than another,
appointing also an order to ordain ministers, which order is clean differ-
ing from the Scriptures; wherefore you must have the order for these
things drawn out of the Scriptures...

I have already made mention of a consistory which were to be had in
every congregation. That consisteth first of the ministers of the same
congregation, as the guides and mouth of the rest, to direct them by the
Scriptures, and to speak at their appointment that which shall be con-
sented upon amongst them all, because of their gifts and place amongst
them, which maketh them more fit for those purposes. The assistants are
they whom the parish shall consent upon and choose for their good
judgment in religion and godliness, using the advice of their ministers
therein chiefly and also using earnest prayers with fasting, as in the
choice of the minister; and having made their choice, thereafter they
shall publish their agreement in their parish... This consistory shall
examine all disordered ceremonies used in place of prayer and abolish
those which they find evil or unprofitable, and bring in such orders as
their congregation shall have need of, so they be few and apparent, necessary both for edifying and profit and decent order...

THOMAS CARTWRIGHT, *The Second Admonition to the Parliament* (1572)

5. Bishops Under Fire
(page 26)

These disputants of ours are so shuffling, and so tenacious of their own opinion, that they will give way to no one who opposes their judgment. . . They are zealously endeavouring to overthrow the entire order of our Anglican Church. Night and day do they importune both the people and the nobility, and stir them up to abhorrence of those persons who, on the abolition of Popery, are faithfully discharging the duties of the ministry, and they busy themselves in everywhere weakening and diminishing their credit. And that they may effect this with greater ease and plausibility, they bawl out to those harpies who are greedily hankering after plunder and spoil, that the property revenues of the cathedral churches ought to be diverted to I know not what other uses. Nor will they allow bishops to take any other precedence than as individual pastors in their respective parishes, whose highest authority they wish to be that of governing, together with their presbytery, the rest of the parishioners. And in this way they set up and establish the equality they speak of. Besides this, they will not acknowledge any government in the Church. They propose, moreover, that the estates and houses of the bishops should be appropriated to pious uses; but, more blind than moles, they do not perceive that they will soon be swallowed up by the devouring wolves. . .

None of the bishops interfere in any matters but the ministry of the word and sacraments, except when the law requires them, or at the command of the sovereign. Nor in these things do they deal harshly with the brethren, but temper what is severe with surprising lenity. Our opponents, however, would complain most grievously were our jurisdiction transferred to the laity : they would soon find out that the gold had been exchanged for brass. But how true are the insinuations which they have whispered against us in the ears of the godly, time will show; and 'our rejoicing is the testimony of our conscience.' I wish they would acquiesce in your wholesome and prudent counsel, namely, to put up with what cannot be amended without great danger. At first they attacked only things of little consequence; but now they turn everything, both great and small, up and down, and throw all things into confusion; and would bring the Church into very great danger, were not our most pious Queen most faithful to her principles, and did she not dread and restrain the vanity and inconsistency of these frivolous men. But because we do not decline to execute the orders of the government, whenever it commands us to interfere, in bridling these our tumultuous brethren, on this ground an undue severity, not to say cruelty, is most unjustly laid to our charge. But we have this one comfort, that the religion of Christ is ever accompanied by the cross, which He will, by His Holy Spirit, enable us willingly to bear.

RICHARD COX, in a letter to Rodolph Gualter (1573)

6. The Lesser Majesty
(page 27)

Concerning the learned exercise and conference amongst the ministers of the Church. I have consulted with divers of my brethren the bishops, who think the same as I do, viz.—a thing profitable to the Church and therefore expedient to be continued. And I trust your Majesty will think the like when your Highness shall be informed of the manner and order thereof; what authority it hath of the Scriptures; what commodity it bringeth with it; and what incommodities will follow if it be clear taken away. . .

I cannot with safe conscience, and without the offence of the Majesty of God, give my consent to the suppressing of these exercises. I choose rather to offend your earthly Majesty than the heavenly Majesty of God. . . In God's matters all princes ought to bow their sceptres to the Son of God, and to ask counsel at His mouth what they ought to do. Remember, Madam, that you are a mortal creature. Must not you also one day appear before the judgment-seat of the Crucified, to receive there what ye have done in the body, whether good or evil? And although ye are a mighty prince, yet remember that He which dwelleth in heaven is mightier.

EDMUND GRINDAL, letter to the Queen (1576)

7. Children's Corner
(page 28)

To the right puissant and terrible priests, my clergy masters of the Confocation-house, whether fickers general, worshipful paltripolitan, or any other of the holy league of subscription...

They are petty popes and petty Antichrists whosoever usurp the authority of pastors over them who by the ordinance of God are to be under no pastors. For none but Antichristian popes and popelings ever claimed this authority unto themselves... Therefore our L. Bps. with the rest of that swinish rabble are petty Antichrists, petty popes, proud prelates, intolerable withstanders of reformation, enemies of the gospel, and most covetous, wretched priests...

Is it any marvel that we have so many swine, dumb dogs, non-residents, with their journeymen the hedge priests, so many lewd livers, as thieves, murderers, adulterers, drunkards, cormorants, rascals, so many ignorant and atheistical dolts, so many covetous popish Bps. in our ministry, and so many and so monstrous corruptions in our Church, and yet likely to have no redress; seeing our impudent, shameless and wainscot-faced bishops ... dare in the ears of her Majesty affirm all to be well where there is nothing but sores and blisters, yea, where the grief is even deadly at the heart?

MARTIN MARPRELATE, *The Epistle* (1588)

8. Keeping the Sabbath
(page 32)

It is most certain that we are commanded to rest from all things which might hinder us from the sanctifying of the Sabbath ... of which sort are all honest recreations and lawful pleasures which are permitted unto us upon the other days to further us in the works of our calling, which we do stand in need of even as of meat and drink and sleep... We must not think it sufficient that we do no work upon the Sabbath, and in the mean season be occupied about all manner of delights, but we must cease as well from the one as from the other. Therefore upon this day all sorts of men must give over utterly all shooting, hunting, hawking, tennis, fencing, bowling or such like, and they must have no more dealing with them than the artificer with his trade or husbandman with his plough.

NICHOLAS BOWNDE, *The Doctrine of the Sabbath* (1595)

9. The Apostolic Church
(page 33)

Concerning their assertion that our form of Church polity is corrupted with Popish orders, rites and ceremonies, banished out of certain reformed Churches, whose example therein we ought to have followed.

Concerning rites and ceremonies, there may be fault either in the kind or in the number and multitude of them. The first thing blamed about the kind of ours is that in many things we have departed from the ancient simplicity of Christ and His Apostles, we have embraced more outward stateliness, we have those orders in the exercise of religion which they who best pleased God and served Him most devoutly never had. For it is out of doubt that the first state of things was best, that in the prime of the Christian religion faith was soundest, the Scriptures of God were then best understood by all men, all parts of godliness did then most abound; and therefore it must needs follow that customs, laws and ordinances devised since are not so good for the Church of Christ, but the best way is to cut off later inventions and to reduce things unto the ancient state wherein at first they were. Which rule or canon we hold to be either uncertain or at leastwise insufficient, if not both. For in case it be certain, hard it cannot be for them to show us where we shall find it so exactly set down that we may say without controversy, *These were the orders of the Apostles' times, these wholly and only, neither fewer nor more than these...*

So that in tying the Church to the orders of the Apostles' times they tie it to a marvellous uncertain rule, unless they require the observation of no orders but only those which are known to be apostolical by the Apostles' own writings. But then is not this their rule of such sufficiency that we should use it as a touchstone to try the orders of the Church by for ever. Our end ought always to be the same; our ways and means thereunto not so. The glory of God and the good of His Church was the thing which the Apostles aimed at and therefore ought to be the mark whereat we also level. But seeing those rites and orders may be at one time more which at other time are less available unto that purpose, what reason is there in these things to urge the state of our only age as a pattern for all to follow? It is not, I am right sure, their meaning that we should now assemble our people to serve God in close and secret meetings; or that common brooks or rivers should be used for places of baptism; or that the Eucharist should be ministered after meat; or that the custom of church-feasting should be renewed; or that all kinds of standing provision for the ministry should be utterly taken away and their estate made again dependent upon the voluntary devotion of men. In these things they easily perceive how unfit that were for the present, which was for the first age convenient enough.

RICHARD HOOKER, *The Laws of Ecclesiastical Polity* (1594)

10. Imperial Advantages
(page 35)

It is honourable, both for that by this means infinite numbers of souls may be brought from their idolatry, bloody sacrifices, ignorance and incivility, to the worshipping of the true God aright to civil conversation; and also their bodies freed from the intolerable tyranny of the Spaniards whereunto they are already or likely in short space to be subjected, unless her excellent Majesty or some other Christian prince do speedily assist and afterward protect them in their just defensive wars against the violence of usurpers. . .

Likewise it is profitable, for hereby the Queen's dominions may be exceedingly enlarged, and this realm inestimably enriched, with precious stones, gold, silver, pearl and other commodities which those countries yield, and (God giving good success to the voyage) an entrance made thereby to many other empires (which happily may prove as rich as this). . .

To be short, all sound Christians do repute the Kings of Castile and Portugal mere usurpers in Africa and America. . . Christians may not warrantably conquer infidels upon pretence only of their infidelity. But I hold it very reasonable and charitable to send preachers, safely guarded if need be, to offer infidels the glad tidings of the Gospel. . .

We may make choice to arm and instruct such of them as we find most trusty and most prone to Christianity, reserving the powder and shot in our own custody. . . Besides this easy and compendious way of possessing Guiana by arming the inhabitants, there is special choice to be had in sending preachers of good discretion and behaviour for their conversion.

SIR WALTER RALEIGH, *The Discovery of Guiana* (1596)

11. Freedom of Trade
(page 39)

The Committees from the House of Commons sat five whole afternoons upon these Bills. There was a great concourse of clothiers and merchants, of all parts of the realm, and especially of London; who were so divided as that all the clothiers, and in effect all the merchants of England, complained grievously of the engrossing and restraint of trade by the rich merchants of London, as being to the undoing or great hindrance of all the rest; and of London merchants, three parts joined in the same complaint against a fourth part; and of that fourth part, some standing stiffly for their own company, yet repined at other companies. . .

Natural Right—All free subjects are born inheritable as to their land, so also to the free exercise of their industry in those trades whereto they apply themselves and whereby they are to live. Merchandise being the chiefest and richest of all other, it is against the natural right and liberty of the subjects of England to restrain it into the hands of some few, as it now is; . . . the mass of the whole trade of all the realm is in the hands of some 200 persons at the most, the rest serving for a show only, and reaping small benefit. . .

Examples of Nations—The example of all other nations generally in the world, who avoid in themselves, and hate in us, this monopolising way of traffic. . .

Wealth—The increase of the wealth generally of all the land by the ready vent of all the commodities to the merchants at higher rate; for where many buyers are, ware grows dearer; and they that buy dear at home must sell dear abroad: this also will make our people more industrious.

Equal Distribution—The more equal distribution of the wealth of the land, which is a great stability and strength to the realm, even as the equal distributing of the nourishment in a man's body; the contrary whereof is inconvenient in all estates, and oftentimes breaks out into mischief when too much fullness doth puff up some by presumption, and too much emptiness leaves the rest in perpetual discontent, the mother of desire of innovations and troubles: and this is the proper fruit of monopolies. Example may be in London and the rest of the realm: The custom and impost of London come to £110,000 a year, and the rest of the whole realm but to £17,000.

Strength—The increase of shipping, and especially of mariners, in all ports of England. How greatly the mariners of the realm have decayed, and with how greater danger of the state in these late wars, is known to them who have been employed in that kind of service; who also do attribute the cause thereof to this restraint of trade; free traffic being the breeder and maintainer of ships and mariners, as by memorable example in the Low Countries may be seen. ..

Necessity at Home—And as there will be greater opportunity abroad, so also much greater necessity at home; for what else shall become of gentlemen's younger sons, who cannot live by arms when there is no wars, and learning preferments are common to all and mean? So that nothing remains fit for them save only merchandise, unless they turn serving-men, which is a poor inheritance.

MEMORANDUM ON A BILL FOR FREE TRADE (1604)

12. Perils of the Dance
(page 42)

For certain it is, the exercise itself, in its own nature, quality and propriety, though to some it is lawful, to other some unlawful in divers respects, is both ancient and general, having been used ever in all ages, as well of the Godly as of the wicked, almost from the beginning. Wherefore, when I condemn the same in some, my meaning is in respect of the manifold abuses thereof. And in my judgment, as it is used nowadays, an Occupation being made of it, and a continual exercise, without any difference or respect had either to time, person, sex or place, in public assemblies and frequencies of people, with such beastly slabberings, kissings and smouchings with other filthy gestures therein accustomed, it is as impossible to be used without doing of infinite hurt as it is for a naked man to lie in the midst of a hot burning fire and not to burn. But these abuses, with other the like (as there be legions more in it) being cut off from the exercise itself, the thing itself remaineth more tolerable in some respects. Or else, if our dances tended, as I have said, to the setting forth of God His glory (as the dances used in preter time did) to draw others to piety and sanctity of life, and to praise and rejoicing in God, to recreate the mind oppressed with some great toil or labour, taken in true virtue and godliness, I would not (being done in the fear of God, men by themselves and women by themselves, for else it is not possible to be without sin) much gainstand it. But I see the contrary is everywhere used, to the great dishonour of God and corruption of good manners, which God amend.

PHILIP STUBBES, *The Anatomy of Abuses* (1583)

13. Divine Right
(page 49)

Although God hath power as well of destruction as of creation or maintenance, yet will it not agree with the wisdom of God to exercise His
power in the destruction of nature, and overturning the whole frame of
things since His creatures were made, that His glory might thereby be the
better expressed. So were he a foolish father that would disinherit or destroy his children without a cause, or leave off the careful education of
them; and it were an idle head that would in place of physic so poison or
phlebotomise the body as might breed a dangerous distemper or destruction thereof. . .

How soon kingdoms began to be settled in civility and policy, then did
kings set down their minds by laws, which are properly made by the king
only, but at the rogation of the people, the king's grant being obtained
thereunto. And so the king became to be *lex loquens*, binding himself by
a double oath to the observation of the fundamental laws of the kingdom. . . So, as every just king in a settled kingdom is bound to observe
that paction made to his people by his laws, in framing his government
agreeable thereto . . . therefore a king governing in a settled kingdom
leaves to be a king, and degenerates into a tyrant, as soon as he leaves off
to rule according to his laws. . . As for my part, I thank God I have ever
given good proof that I never had intention to the contrary, and I am
sure to go to my grave with that reputation and comfort, that never king
was in all his time more careful to have his laws duly observed, and
himself to govern thereafter, than I.

I conclude then this point touching the power of kings with this axiom
of Divinity, that as to dispute what God may do is blasphemy . . . so it is
sedition in subjects to dispute what a king may do in the height of his
power, but just kings will ever be willing to declare what they will do,
if they will not incur the curse of God. I will not be content that my
power be disputed upon, but I shall ever be willing to make the reason
appear of all my doings, and rule my actions according to my laws.

JAMES I, speech to Parliament (1610)

14. The King-in-Parliament
(page 54)

The sovereign power is agreed to be in the King: but in the King is a twofold power—the one in Parliament, as he is assisted with the consent of the whole State; the other out of Parliament, as he is sole and singular, guided merely by his own will. And if of these two powers in the King, one is greater than the other and can direct and control the other, that is *suprema potestas,* the sovereign power, and the other is *subordinata.* It will then be easily proved that the power of the King in Parliament is greater than his power out of Parliament, and doth rule and control it; for if the King make a grant by his letters patent out of Parliament, it bindeth him and his successors; but by his power in Parliament he may defeat and avoid it; and therefore that is the greater power. If a judgment be given in the King's Bench by the King himself, as may be and by the law is intended, a writ of error to reverse this judgment may be sued before the King in Parliament. . . So you see the appeal is from the King out of Parliament to the King in Parliament; the writ is in his name; the rectifying and correcting the errors is by him, but with the assent of the Lords and Commons, than which there can be no stronger evidence to prove that his power out of Parliament is subordinate to his power in Parliament; for in Acts of Parliament, be they laws, grounds or whatsoever else, the act and power is the King's but with the assent of the Lords and Commons, which maketh it the most sovereign and supreme power above all and controllable by none.

JAMES WHITELOCKE, speech on impositions (1610)

15. Rights of the Commons
(page 57)

The Commons now assembled in Parliament, being justly occasioned thereunto concerning sundry liberties, franchises and liberties of Parliament, do make this Protestation following.

That the liberties, franchises, privileges and jurisdictions of Parliament are the ancient and undoubted birthright and inheritance of the subjects of England; and that the arduous and urgent affairs concerning the King, state and defence of the realm, and of the Church of England, and the maintenance and making of laws, and redress of mischiefs and grievances which daily happen within this realm, are proper subjects and matters of counsel and debate in Parliament; and that in the handling and proceeding of those businesses every member of the House of Commons hath, and of right ought to have, freedom of speech to propound, treat, reason and bring to conclusion the same; and that the Commons in Parliament have like liberty and freedom to treat of these matters in such order as in their judgments shall seem fittest; and that every member of the said House hath like freedom from all impeachment, imprisonment and molestation (other than by censure of the House itself) for or concerning any matter or matters touching the Parliament or Parliament business; and that if any of the said members be complained of and questioned for anything done or said in Parliament, the same is to be showed to the King by the advice and assent of all the Commons assembled in Parliament before the King give any credence to any private information.

THE COMMONS' PROTESTATION (1621)

16. Royal Address
(page 59)

These times are for action; wherefore, for example's sake, I mean not to spend much time in words, expecting accordingly that your (as I hope) good resolutions will be speedy, not spending time unnecessarily, or (that I may better say) dangerously, for tedious consultations at this conjuncture of time is as hurtful as ill resolutions.

I am sure you now expect from me both to know the cause of your meeting, and what to resolve on; yet I think there is none here but knows what common danger is the cause of this Parliament, and that supply at this time is the chief end of it; so that I need but to point to you what to do. I will use but few persuasions, for if to maintain your own advices and the true religion, the laws, liberties of this State, and the just defence of our true friends and allies, be not sufficient, no eloquence of men or angels will prevail.

Only let me remember you that my duty most of all, and every one of yours according to his degree, is to seek the maintenance of this Church and Commonwealth; and certainly there was never a time in which this duty was more necessarily required than now.

I, therefore, judging a Parliament to be the ancient, speediest and best way, in this time of common danger, to give such supply as to secure ourselves and to save our friends from imminent ruin, have called you together. Every man now must do according to his conscience, wherefore if you (which God forbid) should not do your duties in contributing what this State at this time needs, I must in discharge of my conscience use those other means which God hath put into my hands to save that that the follies of particular men may otherwise hazard to lose.

Take not this as a threatening (for I scorn to threaten any but my equals) but an admonition from him that, both out of nature and duty, hath most care of your preservations and prosperities, and hopes that your demeanours at this time will be such as shall not only approve your former counsels but lay on me such obligations as shall tie me by way of thankfulness to meet often with you, for be assured that nothing can be more pleasing unto me than to keep a good correspondency with you.

CHARLES I, speech to Parliament (March 1628)

17. A Forthright Queen
(page 59)

I have received your letter by the post, with the message that the Parliament has sent you, which I think is pretty fair, since they believe they can have everything by speaking high words. As to your journey into Ireland, I say nothing about it, having written on that subject before; but as to the discourse you have had about Hull, I must say in truth that to me it is a strange thing that there is anyone who can argue against that, and that you have not attempted to get it already; for the longer you wait, the worse it will be: and [can you] believe that if there come a fleet to fetch away the arms, you will be able to hinder it? If, before that, you do not get the place, the folly is so great that I do not understand it. Delays have always ruined you. As to your answer on the militia, I would believe that you will not consent to pass it for two years, as I understand you will be pressed to do, and that you will refuse it. But perhaps it is already done; you are beginning again your old game of yielding everything. For my own consolation, however, I will hope the contrary, till I hear the decision; for I confess that if you do it, you ruin me in ruining yourself; and that, could I have believed it, I should never have quitted England; for my journey is rendered ridiculous by what you do, having broken all the resolutions that you and I had taken, except of going where you are, and that to do nothing . . . But you have done in this, I am afraid, as you did in the affair of the bishops; for at one time you could have entered into an accommodation about that, and you were obstinate that you would not, and after all you yielded it. Meanwhile I went out of England, contrary to everybody's opinion, and I have made myself ridiculous. . . As for staying in York without doing anything, I might have done that.

Forgive me for writing all this to you: the truth is that I see I shall be constrained by my misfortunes to retire to some place where I can pray to God for you. I understand that they are willing to give you tonnage and poundage for three years. I repeat to you, that if you cannot have it as you ought, that is to say, in your own power to dispose of it, you pass a thing against yourself. . . I send you this express, hoping you will not have passed the Militia Bill. If you have, I must think about retiring for the present into a convent, for you are no longer capable of protecting anyone, not even yourself. Adieu, my dear heart.

HENRIETTA MARIA, letter to Charles I from The Hague (May 1642)

18. Preserving the Constitution
(page 62)

The form of government is that which doth actuate and dispose every
part and member of a state to the common good; and as those parts give
strength and ornament to the whole, so they receive from it again
strength and protection in their several stations and degrees. If this
mutual relation and intercourse be broken, the whole frame will quickly
be dissolved and fall in pieces, and instead of this concord and inter-
change of support, whilst one part seeks to uphold the old form of
government, and the other part to introduce a new, they will miserably
consume and devour one another. Histories are full of the calamities of
whole states and nations in such cases. It is true that time must needs
bring some alterations, and every alteration is a step and degree towards
a dissolution; those things only are eternal which are constant and uniform. Therefore it is observed by the best writers upon this subject that
those commonwealths have been most durable and perpetual which have
often reformed and recomposed themselves according to their first institution and ordinance; for by this means they repair the breaches and
counterwork the ordinary and natural effects of time.

JOHN PYM, speech on the impeachment of Manwaring (1628)

19. A Bibulous Bishop
(page 67)

He was made Bishop of Oxford, and I have heard that he had an admir-
able, grave and venerable aspect.

One time, as he was confirming, the country-people pressing in to see
the ceremony, said he, *Bear off there, or I'll confirm ye with my staff*.
Another time, being to lay his hand on the head of a man very bald, he
turns to his chaplain, Lushington, and said, *Some dust, Lushington* (to
keep his hand from slipping.) There was a man with a great venerable
beard: said the Bishop, *You, behind the beard*.

His chaplain, Dr Lushington, was a very learned and ingenious man
and they loved one another. The Bishop sometimes would take the key
of the wine-cellar, and he and his chaplain would go and lock themselves
in and be merry. Then first he lays down his episcopal hat—*There lies*

the Doctor. Then he puts off his gown—*There lies the Bishop*. Then 'twas, *Here's to thee, Corbet*, and, *Here's to thee, Lushington*.

He married Alice Hutton, whom 'twas said he begot. She was a very beautiful woman, and so was her mother.

JOHN AUBREY, *Brief Lives* (on Richard Corbet, Bishop of Oxford and of Norwich)

20. Wordy Bird
(page 71)

Yesterday I went
To see a lady that has a parrot; my woman,
While I was in discourse, converted the fowl,
And now it can speak naught but Knox's words.
So there's a parrot lost.

JASPER MAYNE, *The City Match* (1639)

21. Thunder on the Left
(page 73)

Though the voice of Christ's reign came first from the multitude; yet it comes but in a confused manner, as the noise of many waters. Though the multitude may begin a thing, and their intention may be good in it, yet it is not for them to bring it to perfection: that which they do commonly is mixed with much confusion and a great deal of disorder. The people had a hint of something: Down with Antichrist, down with Popery. Not understanding distinctly what they did, their voice was but as the voice of many waters. Therefore it follows: *and as the voice of mighty thunderings*. After the beginning of this confused noise among the multitude, God moves the hearts of great ones, of noble, of learned ones; and they come in to the work, and their voice is as the voice of mighty thundering, a voice that strikes terror and hath a majesty in it to prevail. This is the work of the day, for us to lift up our voice to heaven, that it might be mighty to bring forth more and more the voice of our Parliament as a voice of thunder, a terrible voice to the Antichristian party, that they may say, *The Lord God Omnipotent* reigneth. And let us not be discouraged, for our prayers, though they be poor and mean and scattered, they may further the voice of thunderings.

HANSERD KNOLLYS, *A Glimpse of Sion's Glory* (1641)

22. War without an Enemy
(page 76)

The experience I have had of your worth and the happiness I have enjoyed in your friendship are wounding considerations to me when I look upon this present distance between us. Certainly, my affections to you are so unchangeable that hostility itself cannot violate my friendship to your person. But I must be true to the cause wherein I serve. The old limitation *usque ad aras* holds still; and where my conscience is interested, all other obligations are swallowed up. I should most gladly wait upon you, according to your desire, but that I look upon you as engaged in that party beyond the possibility of a retreat, and consequently uncapable of being wrought upon by any persuasion. And I know the conference could never be so close between us but that it would take wind, and receive a construction to my dishonour. That great God who is the searcher of my heart knows with what a sad sense I go upon this service, and with what a perfect hatred I detest this war without an enemy. But I look upon it as sent from God; and that is enough to silence all passion in me. The God of Heaven in good time send us the blessing of peace, and in the mean time fit us to receive it. We are both upon the stage, and must act such parts as are assigned to us in this tragedy. Let us do it in the way of honour, and without personal animosities.

SIR WILLIAM WALLER, in a letter to Sir Ralph Hopton (1643)

(Waller and Hopton had fought together in the Thirty Years War, but the Civil War found them on opposing sides and Hopton had proposed a conference before they met in battle.)

23. The Sovereignty of Conscience
(page 82)

And as for matters of conscience or opinion about religion or worship, with which human society, cohabitation and safety may freely subsist and stand together—that doth not fall under the power of the magisterial sword, either for introduction and settlement, or for extirpation and subversion. For the limits of magistracy extend no further than humanity or human subsistence, not to spirituality or spiritual being; and no further than its own nature extends, no further may its compulsive power be stretched. And this is the true distinction, for matter of subjection, betwixt God and Caesar; and what is God's we must in the first place give unto God, and what is Caesar's, in the second place, freely and readily we must give unto Caesar. The inward man is God's prerogative; the outward man is man's prerogative. God is the immediate Lord over the inward, and mediately over the outward; but man is only lord over the outward, and though immediate thereover, yet by deputation and commission from Him who is thus both over the one and the other. And God, who only knoweth the heart and searcheth the reins, hath reserved the gubernation thereof to Himself as His own prerogative. And the only means which He useth in this kind of government, that by His ministers must be dispensed, is only by the Word, not by the sword.

RICHARD OVERTON, *An Appeal from the Commons to the Free People* (1647)

24. Fundamentals of the Army
(page 83)

Nor will it now, we hope, seem strange or unseasonable to rational and honest men if we shall, before disbanding, proceed in our own and the kingdom's behalf to propound and plead for some provision for our and the kingdom's satisfaction and future security. . . Especially considering that we were not a mere mercenary army, hired to serve any arbitrary power of a state, but called forth and conjured by the several declarations of Parliament to the defence of our own and the people's just rights and liberties. And so we took up arms in judgment and conscience to those ends, and have so continued them, and are resolved . . . to assert and vindicate the just power and rights of this kingdom in Parliament for those common ends premised, against all arbitrary power, violence and oppression, and all particular parties and interests whatsoever; the said declarations still . . . assuring us that all authority is fundamentally seated in the office, and but ministerially in the persons. Neither do or will these our proceedings, as we are fully and in conscience persuaded, amount to anything unwarrantable before God and men; being thus far much short of the common proceedings in other nations, to things of an higher nature than we have yet appeared to. And we cannot but be sensible of the great complaints that have been made to us generally in the kingdom from the people where we march, of arbitrariness and injustice to their great and insupportable oppressions.

DECLARATION OF THE ARMY (14 June 1647)

25. Advice from Preston
(page 84)

Surely, Sir, this is nothing but the hand of God; and wherever anything in this world is exalted, or exalts itself, God will pull it down; for this is the day wherein He alone will be exalted. It is not fit for me to give advice, nor to say a word what use you should make of this, more than to pray you, and all that acknowledge God, that they would exalt Him —and not hate His people, who are as the apple of His eye, and for whom even Kings shall be reproved; and that you would take courage to do the work of the Lord, in fulfilling the end of your magistracy in seeking the peace and welfare of this land,—that all that will live peaceably may have countenance from you, and they that are incapable and will not leave troubling the land may speedily be destroyed out of the land. And if you take courage in this, God will bless you; and good men will stand by you; and God will have glory, and the land will have happiness by you in despite of all your enemies.

OLIVER CROMWELL, to the Speaker of the Commons (1648)

26. A Forbidden Feast
(page 86)

I went to London with my wife, to celebrate Christmas-day, Mr Gunning preaching in Exeter chapel on Micah vii 2. Sermon ended, as he was giving us the Holy Sacrament the chapel was surrounded with soldiers, and all the communicants and assembly surprised and kept prisoners by them, some in the house, others carried away. . . . In the afternoon came Colonel Whalley, Goffe and others, from Whitehall, to examine us one by one; some they committed to the Marshal, some to prison. When I came before them, they took my name and abode, examined me why, contrary to the ordinance made that none should any longer observe the superstitious time of the Nativity (so esteemed by them), I durst offend, and particularly be at Common Prayers, which they told me was but the Mass in English, and particularly pray for Charles Stuart; for which we had no Scripture. I told them we did not pray for Charles Stuart, but for all Christian Kings, Princes and Governors. They replied, in so doing we prayed for the King of Spain too, who was their enemy and a Papist, with other frivolous and ensnaring questions, and much threatening; and finding no colour to detain me, they dismissed me with much pity of my ignorance. These men were of high flight and above ordinances, and spake spiteful things of our Lord's Nativity. As we went up to receive the Sacrament, the miscreants held their muskets against us, as if they would have shot us at the altar; but yet suffering us to finish the office of Communion, as perhaps not having instructions what to do in case they found us in that action.

JOHN EVELYN, *Diary* (for 25 December 1657)

27. Disappointment in a Preacher
(page 87)

God forgive me, I was as near laughing yesterday where I should not:' would you believe I had the grace to go to hear a sermon upon a week-day? In earnest, 'tis true, and Mr Marshall was the man that preached, but never anybody was so defeated. He is so famed that I expected rare things from him, and seriously I listened to him at first with as much reverence and attention as if he had been St Paul. And what do you think he told us? why, that if there were no kings, no queens, no lords, no ladies, no gentlemen or gentlewomen in the world, it would be no loss at all to God Almighty: this he said over some forty times, which made me remember it, whether I would or not. The rest was much at this rate, entertained with the prettiest odd phrases, that I had the most ado to look soberly enough for the place I was in that ever I had in my life. He does not preach so always, sure; if he does, I cannot believe his sermons will do much towards the bringing anybody to heaven more than by exercising their patience; yet I'll say that for him, he stood stoutly for tithes, though in my opinion few deserve them less than he, and it may be he would be better without them.

DOROTHY OSBORNE, in a letter to Sir William Temple (1653)

28. Troubled Saints
(page 89)

There were amongst them some few of the quality and degree of gentle-men, and who had estates, and such a proportion of credit and reputa-tion as could consist with the guilt they had contracted. But much the major part of them consisted of inferior persons, of no quality or name, artificers of the meanest trades, known only by their gifts in praying and preaching; which was now practised by all degrees of men, but scholars, throughout the kingdom. . . . In a word, they were a pack of weak sense-less fellows, fit only to bring the name and reputation of Parliament lower than it was yet. . . .

There were now no bishops for them to be angry with; they had already reduced all that order to the lowest beggary. But their quarrel was against all who had called themselves ministers, and who, by being called so, received tithes, and respect from their neighbours. They resolved the function itself to be antichristian, and the persons to be burdensome to the people, and the requiring and payment of tithes to be absolute Judaism, and they thought fit that they should be abolished altogether. . . .

When they had tired and perplexed themselves so long in such debates, as soon as they were met in the morning upon the twelfth of December, and before many of them were come who were like to dissent from the motion, one of them stood up and declared, 'that he did believe they were not equal to the burden that was laid upon them, and therefore that they might dissolve themselves'.

CLARENDON, *History of the Great Rebellion*

29. Invitation to a Glorious Death
(page 90)

To your Highness justly belongs the honour of dying for the people; and it cannot choose but be unspeakable consolation to you in the last moments of your life to consider with how much benefit to the world you are like to leave it. 'Tis then only (my Lord) the titles you now usurp will be truly yours, you will then indeed be the Deliverer of your country, and free it from a bondage little inferior to that from which Moses delivered his. You will then be that true Reformer which you would be thought. Religion shall be then restored, liberty asserted, and Parliaments have those privileges they have fought for. We shall then hope that other laws will have place besides those of the sword, and that justice shall be otherwise defin'd than the will and pleasure of the strongest, and we shall then hope men will keep oaths again, and not have the necessity of being false and perfidious to preserve themselves, and be like their rulers. All this we hope from your Highness's happy expiration, who are the true Father of your country. . . . Let this consideration arm and fortify your Highness's mind against the fears of death, and the terrors of your evil conscience, that the good you will do by your death will something balance the evils of your life. And if in the black catalogue of High Malefactor, few can be found that have lived more to the affliction and disturbance of mankind than your Highness hath done, yet your greatest enemies will not deny but there are likewise as few that have expired more to the universal benefit of mankind than your Highness is like to do. To hasten this great good is the chief end of my writing this paper; and if it have the effects I hope it will, your Highness will quickly be out of the reach of men's malice.

EDWARD SEXBY, *Killing No Murder* (1657)

30. Dissolution, 1658
(page 93)

I did tell you at a conference concerning it, that I would not undertake it unless there might be some other persons that might interpose between me and the House of Commons, who then had the power, to prevent tumultuary and popular spirits; and it was granted I should name another House. I named it of men that shall meet you wheresoever you go, and shake hands with you; and tell you it is not titles, nor lords, nor party that they value, but a Christian and an English interest. Men of your own rank and quality, who will not only be a balance unto you, but a new force added to you, while you love England and religion ...

It hath been not only your endeavour to pervert the Army while you have been sitting, and to draw them to state the question about a Commonwealth; but some of you have been listing of persons, by commission of Charles Stuart, to join with any insurrection that may be made. And what is like to come upon this, the enemy being ready to invade us, but ever present blood and confusion? And if this be so, I do assign it to this cause: your not assenting to what you did invite me to by the Petition and Advice, as that which might be the settlement of the nation. And if this be the end of your sitting, and this be your carriage— I think it high time that an end be put to your sitting. And I do dissolve this Parliament. And let God be judge between you and me.

OLIVER CROMWELL to the House of Commons (February 1658)

Further Reading

John Aubrey, *Brief Lives*, Secker and Warburg 1969, Penguin 1972.

Clarendon, *History of the Great Rebellion*, Oxford University Press.

Patrick Collinson, *The Elizabethan Puritan Movement*, Cape 1967.

G. R. Elton (ed.), *The Tudor Constitution*, Cambridge University Press 1960.

William Haller, *The Rise of Puritanism*, Columbia University Press 1938.

Christopher Hill, *The Century of Revolution*, 1603–1714, Nelson 1961, Sphere 1969.

Economic Problems of the Church, Oxford University Press 1956, Panther 1971.

God's Englishman: Oliver Cromwell and the English Revolution, Weidenfeld & Nicolson 1970, Penguin 1972.

Puritanism and Revolution, Panther 1968.

A. A. Hillary, *Oliver Cromwell and the Challenge to the Monarchy*, Pergamon Press 1969.

Lucy Hutchinson, *Memoirs of the Life of Colonel Hutchinson*, Dent 1965, Oxford University Press 1973.

J. P. Kenyon (ed.), The Stuart Constitution, 1603–1688, Cambridge University Press 1966.

M. M. Knappen, *Tudor Puritanism*, University of Chicago Press 1966.

W. M. Lamont, *Godly Rule*, Macmillan 1970.

J. E. Neale, *Elizabeth I and her Parliaments*, Cape 1953.

H. C. Porter (ed.), *Puritanism in Tudor England*, Macmillan 1971.

M. M. Reese, *The Tudors and Stuarts*, Edward Arnold 1940.

C. Russell, *The Crisis of Parliaments*, Oxford University Press 1971.

Lawrence Stone, *The Causes of the English Revolution*, Routledge 1972.

The Crisis of the Aristocracy, 1558–1641, Oxford University Press 1965.

J. R. Tanner (ed.), *Constitutional Documents of the Reign of James I*, Cambridge University Press 1960.

R. H. Tawney, *Religion and the Rise of Capitalism*, Murray 1926, Penguin 1969.

H. R. Trevor-Roper, *Archbishop Laud*, Macmillan 1940.

C. V. Wedgwood, *The King's Peace*, Collins 1955, Fontana 1966.

The King's War, Collins 1958, Fontana 1966.

A. S. P. Woodhouse, *Puritanism and Liberty*, Dent 1965.

G. Yule, *The Independents in the English Civil War*, Cambridge University Press 1958.

Index